DR. JUDITH LANDAU
AND JAMES GARRETT

INVITATIONAL INTERVENTION:

A STEP BY STEP GUIDE FOR CLINICIANS HELPING FAMILIES ENGAGE RESISTANT SUBSTANCE ABUSERS IN TREATMENT

2006

To order additional copies, please contact us.
BookSurge, LLC
www.booksurge.com
1-866-308-6235
orders@booksurge.com

To Mary
With many thanks
for your "magic hands"
and delightful
healing presence.

Judith
Jan 2007

Linc
Linking Human Systems™

Invitational Intervention:

A Step-by-Step Guide

For Clinicians Helping

Families Engage Resistant

Substance Abusers in Treatment

ARISE

A Relational Intervention
Sequence for Engagement

Dedication

*T*he Authors Wish To Dedicate This Book To The Many Addicted Individuals And Their Families, Who Initiated The Process Of Recovery, And From Whom We Have Learned And Continue To Learn So Much.

Acknowledgements

The authors wish to thank Marcia Larabee, Mable Stewart, and Anna Weaver for their thoughtful edits, late night dedication, and numerous insightful suggestions that have greatly improved the book.

A special thanks to Mable for coordinating the project, and to Anna for incorporating her "technical" expertise into the manuscript where appropriate. We are also grateful to Heather Outlaw for reading the rough manuscript and contributing her wisdom to the final product.

This step-by-step guide incorporates a wealth of research, both of the authors and of many of their colleagues. In order not to distract the reader from its primary purpose as a "How To" book, the author's made the very difficult decision to withhold the references from the text, and instead to include them in an expansive bibliography and suggested reading list at the end of the book.

For those readers who wish to pursue the detailed references and connect the appropriate material to them, please refer to the peer-reviewed published ARISE and Resilience papers referenced in the Bibliography and also available on our website at www.linkinghumansystems.com.

TABLE OF CONTENTS

PREFACE

Our work has grown from our many years of experience of working with addicted persons and their families, and all they have taught us about resilience, hope and healing. In this book we will share our philosophy of addiction, describe the underlying philosophy and principles of our approach to working with families, and why we believe that an invitational form of Intervention is vastly superior to coercion. We entered the addiction field through very different channels, and our working collaboratively combines the biopsychosocial, or mind-body-spirit approach of our vastly different, shared cultural experiences.

Our Entry Into the Field of Addiction
Judith

Raised in multicultural South Africa, Judith was strongly influenced by the tribal structure, traditional healers and intergenerational storytelling of the African tribes, as well as the strengths of the extended family structure of Indian, Italian, and Portuguese families, to mention only a few of the many cultures comprising the colorful and exciting landscape of her homeland. The religions to which she was exposed ranged from beliefs in Buddhism, to the Judeo-Christian-Muslim faiths, to the praying mantis and the antelope deities of the Bushmen. Spirituality and communication with "the other side" was taken for granted. It was no surprise to hear that a Bushman needed to travel many hundreds of miles to visit a sick relative because the beating of his heart had given him a message to do so, or to hear that a major rift between a Zulu woman and her mother-in-law had been healed because a deceased ancestor had appeared and ordered that the fighting cease for the sake of the grandchildren.

The death of Judith's father as a result of political oppression when she and her brother were still young children, led to her discovering first hand the importance of blood and non-blood ties of the larger support system. Jim, while growing up in Upstate New York, where his colleagues were more comfortable with a nuclear family model and the rather narrower religious beliefs of those who originated in, or had immigrated to, his area in the United States, had his own roots in the Seneca Nation, and easily understood Judith's larger systems perspective and her belief in the importance of context and intergenerational influences.

Judith, while a very young and naïve psychiatric resident, with no experience or knowledge of addiction——other than the whispered hints that her maternal grandfather, having deserted his seven surviving children to try to retrieve money from his debtors, might have died on the London streets as a broken alcoholic after losing his wife, his fortune and his reputation following the economic depression and ostrich feather slump of World War I——was sent to direct a large addiction hospital.

This was her punishment for seeing the parents and families of troubled children and adolescents in the mid-sixties, rather than working solely with the children, leaving their "collateral members" to the "more appropriate" responsibility of the nurses and social workers. Working with families was not yet an accepted form of therapy. As an alternative to being dismissed from the residency at the request of those deprived of their "appropriate" roles, she was given the option of, "Go run the Addiction Service where you can do no good since nobody ever gets better anyway; but you probably can't do any harm either!"

Knowing no better, and determined to learn whatever she could about this exciting new field of addiction, she invited into the treatment setting all those from whom she thought she could learn: members of the extended family, the employers, the teachers, the neighbors, the primary care providers, and whoever else was available from the patient's support system. The only known successful treatment system at that time was Alcoholics Anonymous, so she invited them to hold meetings in the hospital, and learned from their meetings as well. The staff, patients and family members of the William Slater Hospital, Cape Town, South Africa, proved to be one of the best training environments anyone could ever have requested.

Whenever someone from the support system called for an appointment to help a loved one who refused to seek treatment, or who had a history of multiple failed treatments and relapses, Judith instructed the telephone receptionist to encourage that person to come in to talk with her. She had no idea that this was not acceptable practice, or that one should "wait for the addicted person to make the appointment him or herself." With a little encouragement and gentle coaching by Judith through the anxiety, concern and resistance of the caller, the hospital receptionist proved to be an amazing resource at getting resistant substance abusers into treatment.

In fact, the receptionist was able to get her own husband into treatment for the first time in 35 years. Struggling with the painful experience of the confrontational model of the Tavistock analytical group experience——at that time the only group therapy method offered in addiction services——Judith asked her telephone receptionist and her husband to work with her to form a couples group based on their resilience, competence and love for each other. She thought that by their sharing their story of how he had started to abuse alcohol as a result of major intergenerational losses in his family, others might realize that they were not "all bad and hopeless" either, and that there might be hope for their recovery as well.

Together, in 1966, they formed the nucleus of what appears to have been the very first Couples Group for addiction. With that initial success, the rest of the extended families became involved, so that they too could start to experience the positive benefit of viewing addiction from a perspective of competence and resilience, rather than guilt, blame and shame. Thus began the first Multi-Family Groups for Addiction. Social groups were held on Friday nights, and to everyone's amazement, patients who had struggled with their addiction for many years entered and continued in recovery. Naturally, there were episodes of relapse, and it was not unusual for "dagga plants" (the local form of marijuana) plants to be found growing in the garden. Overall, the results were positive and the patients, families, as well as the staff continued to learn.

The lessons Judith learned at the William Slater Hospital, combined with her experience of growing up with the strengths and stresses of a multi-cultural society in times of political and economic distress, formed the basis of her theory of working with people struggling with addiction——Transitional Family Therapy, the model underlying ARISE, the Invitational Intervention about which this book is written.

Jim
Jim grew up in an Irish-Catholic family with a large extended family

system in Rochester, New York. He notes that family gatherings were frequently times when drinking would be an integral part of the social fabric. He remembers discussions between his parents regarding hiding the bottles when certain family members would visit so that there would not be heavy drinking. He remembers his parent's surprise when one of these individuals would end up intoxicated despite the bottles being hidden and no-one having seen that person drinking. Nobody could figure out where he got the alcohol from, and when he could have drunk so much as to have become so obviously intoxicated.

This was Jim's first introduction to alcoholism, and the lessons he learned from this cunning, baffling and powerful disease. Unfortunately, three uncles he loved died from complications related to alcoholism because the family did not know what to do. So, it only seemed natural that Jim would be interested in learning anything he could to help families further their interest to get addicts into recovery. This led Jim to pursue a course of study in Social Work where during two entire years of graduate courses approximately five hours were spent addressing addiction and addiction treatment.

After graduate school, Jim began working in the addictions treatment field, primarily with individuals mandated into treatment due to "Driving While Intoxicated" (DWI) convictions. He learned plenty about denial, resistance, ambivalence, and the importance of families as sources of information and motivation to change. In the mid-1970's, Jim completed a training course to become a Johnson Interventionist and began doing classical Johnson Interventions.

Over the course of the next ten years, he did over 100 interventions and began keeping a record of anecdotal outcomes. Over the course of those 10 years, he observed that the Johnson Intervention was very successful at getting individuals into treatment. Surprisingly however, he learned that most families refused to do an Intervention when they learned what they would need to do, and what the confrontation would involve. It was comfortable for Jim to focus on the positive outcome from Interventions he had done and uncomfortable to look at the fact that the majority of families interested in getting a loved one into treatment refused to do an Intervention.

During the early to mid 1980's these families who refused to do an Intervention were labeled "enablers," "co-dependents," or being, "in denial." There was a general sense that something was wrong with the families——they were to blame for not following through with an Intervention. Jim also observed that most treatment agencies who got calls from family members wanting help to get a loved one into treatment were referred to Al-Anon, even though Al-Anon is not designed for that purpose.

Blaming families who did not follow through with an Intervention and referring individuals who called to get an addicted loved one into treatment to Al-Anon did not make sense to Jim. He began to think that something might be wrong with the method, not with the families who had trouble with the method. Sub-consciously, Jim was observing his own family and what would have worked had they been offered a method to intervene with the alcoholic family members. Subsequently, Jim has seen a number of his family get into recovery as the result of their families being involved in the treatment and recovery process.

Jim and Judith
In the mid-1980's Jim began to work with Judith on the transition of an outpatient addictions treatment agency from an individually based to a systemically based focus. His beliefs about the origins of addiction and the power of families to make a difference took on new meaning by changing the Intervention model from one of secrecy, surprise and coercion to one of openness, no secrecy and invitation. This collaborative work of Jim and Judith resulted in a new method of Intervention that many more families agreed to use because of the attention it paid to their investment in connectedness and the recognition of the inherent competence and health of families. This new method was formalized in the early 1990's as ARISE, the Invitational InterventionTM through which this book will lead you, "Step by Step."

After using the method in their clinical settings in Albany and Rochester, Jim and Judith and their team were able to test the protocol through a research project funded by the National Institute on Drug Abuse (NIDA). The development of Invitational Intervention and other protocols that grew from Transitional Family Theory and Therapy led Judith and Jim to believe that these methods should be made available to individuals, families and communities around the world where they could really be useful. Judith took early retirement from her academic position as professor of psychiatry and family medicine and Director of the Division of Family Programs at the University of Rochester and together they developed the vehicles for doing this: Linking Human Systems, LLC, and LINC Foundation, Inc. (see back materials for more information).

CHAPTER 1
OVERVIEW OF ARISE

The ARISE method——A Relational Intervention Sequence of Engagement——mobilizes family members to motivate Addicted Individuals (AIs) who have been resistant to treatment, or have relapsed many times, to get into treatment and/or self-help. The method was inspired by the authors' explicit belief in the inherent competence and resilience of families. Since both authors grew up in varied cultural backgrounds, and have had many years working professionally in the addiction field, they became progressively convinced that family competence was a crucial factor in addiction recovery.

Through their combined clinical experience, supported by qualitative studies, the authors had also discovered that major, unpredictable, or unresolved loss and grief were key events in the etiology of addiction. They both felt discouraged by the perspective prevalent in the addiction field of the family transmission of addictive disease being inevitable, and the way that this popularly held perspective seemed to contribute to many addicted individuals and their families giving up hope, and becoming overwhelmed by feelings of shame, blame, and guilt.

They learned that this dynamic has kept many AIs from entering treatment, and if anything, serves as a deterrent to treatment engagement. They decided to combine their efforts to work toward mobilizing family strengths to increase the rates of treatment engagement. For greater detail on the authors' paths to this decision, please read their personal introductory statements to this book.

ARISE: A Brief Introduction to the Three Levels
Level I: The First Call
Level I, The First Call, uses motivational techniques designed specifically for telephone coaching, but which can also be applied in face-to-face sessions. Level I is set in motion when the First Caller or Concerned Other (CO) reaches out to a treatment agency or individual

treatment provider for assistance in getting a resistant, addicted loved one into treatment. The First Caller or CO subsequently becomes the "Family Link"—a person who serves as a bridge between the ARISE Invitational Interventionist and the extended family support system.

During Level I, clinicians help the CO establish a basis of hope; identify whom to invite to the initial Intervention meeting; design a strategy to mobilize the support group or Intervention Network; teach techniques to successfully invite the addicted individual (AI) to the first meeting; develop a Recovery Message to be used as part of the invitation; and get a commitment from all potential participants who have been invited to attend the initial meeting, regardless of whether or not the AI attends.

The Recovery Message, typically built around the reconnection of the family transitional pathway, explicitly states the understanding of where the addiction in the family started, and the intent to stop the addiction from progressing into future generations. This is a crucial idea to convey to the addicted individual because it shows that the family does not blame him/her, that they recognize that the entire family needs to heal, and that the individual is not expected to do this alone.

Level I, the First Call, ends after the first meeting if the AI attends and agrees to enter treatment. Once the AI enters treatment, regardless of whether or not s/he attended the first meeting, the ARISE Intervention Network changes focus and continues to meet to: (a) address early recovery ambivalence issues; (b) encourage continuation in treatment, and (c) establish accountability related to ongoing commitment to recovery goals. If the AI does not enter treatment, the Intervention Network goes on to Level II meetings, continuing to invite the AI to each subsequent meeting.

Level II: Strength in Numbers

In Level II, between one to five face-to-face sessions are held with the Intervention Network, with or without the AI present. These meetings are designed to mobilize the group and focus on the goal of treatment engagement.

During these meetings, motivational strategies are developed that are specifically matched to the AI's resistance and his/her reaction to previous attempts to get him/her into treatment. Strategies evolve over the course of these sessions, and the Intervention Network typically develops greater strength as a group, allowing it to deliver a consistent message to the AI that the addiction will no longer run the show and that continued drug and/or alcohol use will not be tolerated.

The reader might think of the Intervention Network in the Level II meetings as the family's "Board of Directors," a powerful group that is brought in to problem solve and break the isolated one-on-one interaction with the AI. This strategy draws on the cohesion of the Intervention Network to show the AI that its members will no longer tolerate a divide and conquer approach. The group speaks in unison and delivers the same Recovery Message repeatedly in order to motivate the AI to enter treatment.

Level III: The Formal ARISE Intervention

Very few families (less than 2%) need to proceed to Level III, the formal ARISE Intervention. In Level III, family and friends set stricter limits and consequences for the AI, still expressed in a loving and supportive way, and put in place only if the AI continues to refuse to enter treatment. By the time the Intervention Network gets to this point, the AI has been given and refused many opportunities to enter treatment. Because the AI has been invited to each of the meetings in both Levels I and II (and may even have attended a number of them), this final limit setting approach is a natural consequence, does not come as a surprise, and is the end of a logical progression of attempts by the Intervention Network to initiate treatment engagement.

By Level III, the Intervention Network is functioning as a support group for all its members, who are able to implement new boundary setting and consequences with the AI, while continuing to offer consistent support for the individual getting into treatment. If the AI enters treatment at this point, the Intervention Network continues to meet to address early recovery ambivalence issues, to encourage continuation in treatment and to establish accountability related to ongoing commitment to the recovery goals. If the AI does not enter treatment, the Intervention Network continues to meet as a support for each other and to foster family recovery.

Treatment Engagement

Do you know that treatment engagement has been identified as a major problem around the world, particularly in the United States? Fewer than 90-95% of substance abusers anywhere in the world receive treatment or attend self-help. Meanwhile, the total cost of drug and alcohol abuse in the United States——including medical care, premature death, unemployment, criminal justice involvement, and addiction treatment——is estimated at over $165 billion and claims 50,000 lives per year. Addiction treatment has been shown to save $7 for every $1 spent. Despite these statistics, apart from Employee Assistance Programs (EAPs) and criminal justice initiatives, very little has been done to increase the number of addicted individuals (AIs) receiving treatment.

Common Myths

A prevailing myth in the addiction field is the belief that addicted individuals (AIs) are "cut off" from their families and that families can be detrimental to their recovery process. To most people's astonishment, however, it has been shown that an AI has *contact that is more frequent* with his/her family than the average person. Throughout this book, the authors illustrate how the family's inherent resilience as well as their capacity and commitment to heal, regardless of the severity of the illness, can be the most important factor in recovery.

Another myth is that the only successful entry point to treatment is a request for care by the addicted person him/herself. However, the frequent contact and close connectedness between AIs and their families provide a potent avenue for engagement through the actions of Concerned Others (COs) such as family, friends, clergy, neighbors, employers, teachers, athletic coaches, school nurses, colleagues, family doctors, and other members of the social support network.

In many addiction agencies/services, when a CO calls for advice about the AI's problem behavior, or seeks help with getting him/her into treatment, typical responses include: "Please have the substance abuser him/herself call," or "We can offer you counseling and support if you come to our Co-Dependents group." The agency will often recommend that the caller attend Al-Anon even though Al-Anon is designed to help family members deal with——and if necessary detach from——the disease of addiction, rather than for the purpose of engaging their loved one in treatment. Al-Anon may provide help and support for the CO, but will not address the AI's need for timely intervention.

Yet another myth is that individuals must "hit bottom" in order to recover successfully. The authors believe that waiting for an individual to "hit bottom" with an addiction is like waiting for a car to break down before taking it to a mechanic to get the problem diagnosed and fixed. Addiction is much like most other medical problems; the earlier the problem can be diagnosed and treated, the better the chance for recovery. Think of how the survival rates of some cancers have increased over recent years. Some of this success can be attributed to the enormous media campaign that has so successfully promulgated the importance of early detection and treatment. Addiction treatment is very similar; the earlier the addiction is treated, the more the individual has to gain because s/he has not yet lost everything. Looking at addiction treatment in this way helps to understand that there really is no "bottom" and certainly no need to wait for an AI to get worse before anything is done to help.

Often, family members fall into behavior patterns of dealing one-on-one with the AI, believing the myth that this is the most effective way of helping the person change. One of the destructive features of addiction is how masterful the AI can be at splitting the family and getting individual family members to talk only on a one-on-one basis. The AI makes promises, uses guilt, and skillfully plays one family member against another in this process.

The authors' research shows that dealing one-on-one with the addicted person is seldom helpful or successful at getting the individual to stop using. In fact, this dynamic is the one most family members give as the reason they feel so angry, frustrated, and ready to give up. Mobilizing other family members is a proven way to stop this destructive influence of addiction. There is strength in numbers and this strength brings with it new hope. With the ARISE method, no longer does any family member have to deal one-on-one with the addicted person.

What is Intervention?

The basic idea behind any intervention is a desire by family, friends, and other concerned members of the support network to take an active role in assisting another person to change unacceptable or self-destructive behavior. The idea of intervention has been around as long as one person has tried to influence the behavior of another. Everyone has been involved in some form of intervention with others. Perhaps one has tried to help a friend who is chronically late getting to work on time; prompted someone who often was erratic about taking prescriptions to take his/her medications on a regular basis; or tried to get a loved one started in an exercise program to help with weight loss.

These are examples of a simple intervention where one person is working to motivate another to change a behavior. This type of intervention is a frequent, daily occurrence. It is usually informal, focused on one objective, and based on the emotional connections and personal relationships directed towards motivating change.

The use of the word Intervention in this book is defined as a formalized process of action taken by Concerned Others (COs) such as family, friends, employers, colleagues, neighbors and co-workers to actively assist someone to change unacceptable behaviors.

ARISE and Stages of Change

ARISE is a three-level Invitational InterventionTM method designed to harness the immense energy and driving force behind Family Motivation to Change®; provide encouragement to mobilize the support system, herein referred to as Intervention Network; and begin the process of an Invitational Intervention with the goal of getting a resistant AI started in treatment. The addicted individual (AI) is "invited" into the process, without secrecy or initial confrontation, but with openness, love, and concern. ARISE maximizes the effort of the family (defined for this purpose as the members of the natural support system), while minimizing the need for considerable time and effort on the part of the professional.

The guiding principle is to stop at the first level that is successful at getting the AI into treatment in order to maximize cost-effectiveness, and to lessen the suffering of the family. The authors believe that Family Motivation to Change is the primary factor that frees the AI to move through Prochaska and DiClemente's Six Stages of Change (Chapter 3, fig. 1) from "Pre-contemplation" into "Contemplation" and then into "Action" to enter recovery. Family Motivation to Change activates Individual Motivation to Change, thereby increasing the likelihood of long-term recovery.

ARISE is one of the few Intervention methods that not only is manual-driven, but also has been formally investigated in a research study funded by the National Institute on Drug Abuse (NIDA). The method and outcome data have been published in peer-reviewed journals and it is viewed as an "Evidence-Based" or "Best Practice" method.

The ARISE Interventionist, the First Caller/Concerned Other/ Family Link, the Addicted Individual, and the Intervention Network

The active participants in the Invitational Intervention are (1) the *ARISE Interventionist*—the addiction professional; (2) the *First Caller/ Concerned Other/Family Link—the concerned other who initially contacts the addiction agency, and who serves as a "Link" between the family and the agency*; (3) the Intervention Network—the AI's support network; *and (4) the Addicted Individual (AI).*

The ARISE Interventionist:

The clinician serving as ARISE Interventionist follows the three-level ARISE protocols in the process of conducting an Invitational Intervention. The ARISE Interventionist coaches the Concerned Other/ Family Link to mobilize the social support system, comprised of family and additional concerned others, to become an Intervention Network with the primary goal of motivating the Addicted Individual to enter treatment or self-help. Part I of this book provides the background and rationale to enable the ARISE Interventionist to coach and educate the Intervention Network. Part II leads the ARISE Interventionist, Step-by-Step, through the Invitational Intervention process.

First Caller serving as Concerned Other/Family Link:

The First Call process depends on the emergence of one person who has the energy, courage and confidence to reach out to an addiction service or professional requesting help for a loved one. This initial drive has to be followed up with the interest, commitment, and willingness to mobilize the rest of the family and natural support system in order to develop the Intervention Network.

ARISE relies on one individual, generally the First Caller, to take the initiative for change. This differs from other intervention methods, which require that the individual with the addiction make the call. ARISE, however, views the First Caller/Concerned Other as a valuable resource in getting the AI into treatment, as opposed to viewing the caller involvement as co-dependent or enabling. The First Caller is the person who, acting on behalf of the Addicted Individual as a Concerned Other, provides the "Link" between the family and the agency to initiate change.

The use of a Family Link to form a bridge between the ARISE Interventionist and the extended family and natural support system allows for true empowerment of the family. Family Links have been shown to serve well in many situations involving chronic and/or life threatening illness or trauma as well as succeeding in addiction interventions. The ARISE trained Interventionist shows his/her commitment and trust by believing that the family has inherent strengths and is capable of overcoming its difficulties by accessing these strengths and resources. This is radical thinking for many of us trained as mental health professionals and may require a new way of viewing clients as our source for the solution by which they will most benefit. It frequently takes what the authors refer to in training as, "A Leap of Faith."

The collaborative relationship that is formed relies on the implicit notion that the family is the expert on itself and its problems. The ARISE Interventionist is the expert in understanding the interface of addiction and the complexity of family relationships. Thus, the family is trusted to do much of the work on its own with solid guidance, but minimal direct involvement, from the ARISE Interventionist.

The Concerned Other, serving as Family Link, needs to be able to access the majority of family members, to be respected by and hold influence with them, and to have no hidden agendas or coalition loyalties. Most families are able to identify this individual without too much difficulty or disagreement. The ARISE Interventionist coaches the First Caller to gain an understanding of the role of Family Link, to make a commitment to the role and tasks required, and to encourage him/her to trust him/herself to be effective.

There are also times when Co-Family Links/Co-COs are required, e.g., when two members of the family share this responsibility. Typically this occurs when the AI is a member (through birth or marriage) of two separate family systems, which might include those recently divorced, newly re-married, warring or inadequately-joined family members. Co-COs/Links are also used when the First Caller is a professional, for example in an emergency room or a primary care service, or an employer or co-worker who does not know the family well.

During the First Call, the ARISE Interventionist employs coaching techniques in order to empower the CO to mobilize and impact the entire family system. In addition to serving as the go-between for the purpose of reducing stressful issues and clarifying discussion points, the CO carries out much of the "real world" logistical coordination of the Intervention process. Typically, the CO's responsibilities may include: (1) coordination and notification of meetings (date, time, place); (2) coordination of payment; (3) informing absent ARISE Intervention Network members of content, topics, and decisions made during meetings, and (4) research of possible treatment options and insurance benefits available for the AI.

Concerned Others (COs) have a powerful stake in resolving identified problems. With minimal coaching, they are capable of mobilizing the extended family and social support networks for problem solving. The results of the NIDA study (see Chapter 1, figure 1) show the success of the CO at engaging resistant AIs in treatment, as a startling example of how, with adequate coaching and a solid support system, Family Links serving as COs can actually achieve better results than professionals.

The Intervention Network

The Concerned Other initiates the first meeting of the ARISE Intervention Network, an extended support group of family members, friends, colleagues, neighbors, clergy, and treating professionals who agree to meet with the express purpose of helping the AI enter treatment. It may also be comprised of step-parents or adult children whose parents and extended families did not approve of their marriages and have therefore not successfully negotiated the "permission to marry" life cycle stage."

The research on ARISE demonstrates a correlation between the size of the Intervention Network and the likelihood that the AI will enter treatment: the larger the network the greater the likelihood of treatment entry. This correlation is based on the following factors:

- The more people involved, the greater the leverage and influence for bringing about change. There is "strength in numbers."

- Frequently, certain members of the network are involved in intense disagreements with the AI. If these members are the only ones present, conversation is likely to become negative and unproductive. A larger network is more likely to maintain focus on treatment entry, avoiding diversion into one-on-one conflicts and old counterproductive history.

- A larger Intervention Network has far greater potential than, for example, a two-person meeting, to generate creative ideas and solve problems. It makes sense that the more minds that are brought to bear on the problem, the more suggestions and innovative solutions will emerge.

- The Intervention Network is encouraged to decide early on in the ARISE process that all decisions regarding the AI will be made by consensus. This "singular voice" prevents the AI from pressuring particular members one-on-one (either in a meeting or on the outside). This prevents anyone from feeling isolated and, therefore, vulnerable in his/her dealings with the AI.

- A larger network is able to dissipate the negative energy induced by ongoing blame, shame and guilt. Invariably, the AI has blamed some family members for his/her past and current situation who, in turn, may have taken on feelings of shame and guilt themselves. A large network can serve as a reminder, not only of the particular strengths and resources, but also of the resilience and survival of the intergenerational family across time. The presence of older family members and children an enhance this perspective and children are sometimes included specifically for this component of the Invitational Intervention process. This positive energy is able to turn negative, hopeless, and destructive situations around. The blame is replaced by an understanding of the original losses from which the substance abuse started; despair is replaced by hope, and frustration is replaced by a plan of action to get the AI into treatment.

- The larger the Intervention Network, the broader the base

of support each member has for one another when the process becomes intense or challenging. No one likes to feel alone in a stressful situation and it often takes a heightened amount of pressure from the Intervention Network to help the AI grasp the seriousness of the problem and accept the need for treatment.

The AI, if present at the meeting, is considered an active participant in the Intervention as opposed to other methods that do not employ *Invitational* Intervention. The AI is provided with options and invited to choose the level at which the intervention proceeds, the type of treatment (in or out-patient), and the ultimate consequences. Given that the AI is kept apprised of all that happens in the process, the choices along the way belong to the AI, even in the event of not choosing to belong.

ARISE Results

A recent non-randomized clinical trial of the ARISE Invitational Intervention showed that following the family initiating the ARISE method 83% (n=91) of 110 severely addicted and resistant alcoholics and substance abusers enrolled in treatment (n=86) or attended self-help meetings (n=5). In cumulative terms, 55% entered treatment in Level I; another 26% were engaged in Level II, bringing the total to 81%. Level III added another 2%, completing the final figure of 83%. The AI's preferred substance did not have any impact on engagement rate, nor did it impact the level of the intervention at which engagement occurred.

Outcome Graph

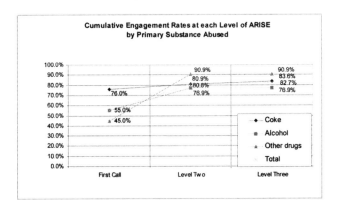

Half of those who entered treatment did so within one week of the Concerned Other contacting an agency or Interventionist. By the end of two weeks, 76% of those who eventually entered treatment had done so, and 86% had entered by the end of week three. The engagement rate did not differ across demographic variables such as age, gender, or race.

Finally, the study showed that ARISE Interventionists averaged less than an hour and a half coaching the First Caller and family members to mobilize their network to motivate the AI to enter treatment. The authors understand that before it can be claimed with more certainty that the engagement numbers are reliable, a randomized clinical trial and replication of the study by other investigators would be desirable.

CHAPTER 2
Why an Invitation?

The idea of inviting an addicted individual (AI) to attend a meeting about a problem s/he believes does not exist, would seem an inevitable prescription for failure. Alternatively, not offering the invitation and proceeding to have a secret meeting without the AI, or springing a surprise meeting on the AI (or telling him/her that s/he had to, or would not be permitted to, attend the meeting), would almost definitely initiate a defiant, rebellious response from having been excluded, talked about, or bossed around. The old adage applies, "Tell me what to do and I will do the exact opposite." The question of why to invite an AI to attend a meeting where the problem of alcohol and drug use will be discussed rests on our understanding that no one—especially an addict—likes to be told what to do.

The authors thoroughly researched this question of invitation. They did a retrospective analysis of some 350 individuals admitted to an Intensive Outpatient Program (IOP) for addiction treatment. These individuals met three evenings each week for sixteen weeks. The study sample was divided according to three significant dynamics that had motivated the AI to start treatment: 1) self-referral, 2) court mandate, and 3) Johnson Intervention.

This retrospective analysis examined the rates of treatment completion and relapse during the course of treatment. The lowest treatment completion rate (40%) was in the self-referred population. The highest completion rate (91%) was in the court-mandated group. The Johnson Intervention group completion rate was 55%. It is interesting to note that the group that appeared to have had the best motivation at the start of treatment (self-referred) had the highest treatment dropout rate. The authors further studied the self-referred group in an attempt to understand this apparent contradiction. They found that the high dropout rate was directly related to the lack of a consequence for dropping out. This self-referred group had no one, other than themselves, to be accountable to when deciding to leave treatment.

At the other end of the spectrum, the court mandated group had the most immediate consequence for dropping out of treatment and, therefore, the highest treatment completion rate. The Johnson Intervention group started off strong in treatment, but had high rates of dropping out after eight to ten weeks. The dynamics of relapse may explain the timing of the Johnson Intervention group's dropout rate with relapses occurring between the sixth and eighth week of treatment.

Dropout rates increased as relapses occurred. During follow-up interviews with the Johnson Intervention group, the authors heard a familiar statement over and over. "At first, I stopped my drug and alcohol use because of the pressure from the Intervention, but then I found myself thinking 'I'm not going to be told what to do!' so I started using again." This finding led the authors to wonder whether the rebellious response and subsequent pattern of relapse noted in the Johnson Intervention group could be avoided by using a method that started with an invitation rather than by surprise or coercion.

Another study by the authors in the 1980's further bolstered their rationale for starting ARISE with an *Invitational* meeting. Data collected from all calls from family members requesting help to get an addicted loved one into treatment revealed that more than eight of every ten families refused to follow through with a Johnson Intervention (the only model being offered at the time). Following this early study, other research has resulted in similar findings. For example, in 1997, Barber and Gilbertson reported that 100% of the women in their Australian study refused to do a Johnson Intervention when it was offered.

Based on these findings, the authors conducted a qualitative study exploring the unwillingness to participate in the Johnson Intervention. They interviewed a sample of families who had refused to do a Johnson Intervention. Some of the reasons the families gave:

- Belief that the kind of support that they were giving the AI was more important or effective than developing or implementing harsh consequences
- Hierarchical respect for a loved one (an adult child for a parent, or a younger sibling for an older sibling)

- Fear that the AI would "go over the edge" if strongly confronted
- Fear that the highly confrontational aspects of the method would destroy the relationship they had with the AI and/or chase him/her away forever
- Fear of reprisal by the AI
- Reluctance and inability to involve others in the Intervention due to their own fears about confrontation
- Skepticism that any method would work, deriving from the family's sense of isolation, confusion, and despair from living for a long time with active addiction

Taking these concerns into account, and understanding that families are motivated to take action or they would not have called asking for help, the authors developed the ARISE Method—A Relational Intervention Sequence of Engagement—as an *Invitational Intervention*.

To clarify the method for both professionals and families, the authors developed a set of operational assumptions that guide the three Levels of the ARISE protocols: 1) The First Call; 2) Strength in Numbers, and 3) The Formal ARISE Intervention (see Chapter 1). The following section explains the seven ARISE Assumptions and gives several case examples from the ARISE research study to demonstrate key points. The case examples also demonstrate the different roles of the First Caller or Concerned Other (CO) in relation to the AI as shown in the table below that was taken from the NIDA research on ARISE.

Relationship of First Caller or Concerned Other to the Addicted Individual (n=94)

Relationship of First Caller or Concerned Other to the Addicted Individual (n=94)

Parent	38	40.3%
Spouse/Partner	29	30.9%
Child	4	4.3%
Misc. Relative	18	19.2%
Non-relative	5	5.3%

ARISE Assumption 1. Involving the addicted individual in the Intervention process as an active participant from the beginning

conveys respect for that person and encourages openness within the overall system.

By the time a family member calls asking for help getting an AI into treatment, there has usually been a long history of manipulation, lying, blaming others, and avoidance by the addict. The family often feels a sense of impotence and despair from living with the addiction. The end products are isolation, secrecy, guilt, and mutual blaming. The natural strengths and resilience of the family have been obscured and compromised.

ARISE supports the family in breaking the AI's control by joining together to open up the topic for discussion and problem solving. This openness begins a rebuilding of the lost respect and trust caused by the addiction. Family members begin to understand that the chaos and dysfunction they have lived with has actually served a purpose and, when carefully explored, has a predictable pattern———a substance abuse pattern that seemed inexplicable when looked at solely in the context of the nuclear family can make perfect sense when viewed over two, three or even more generations of family history, particularly when viewed in the light of cultural, economic, geological, and political events that might have occurred during those times.

Case Example
Parent Intervenes with an Adult Child

In this case, the network decided to establish a firm consequence with treatment added as a second condition.

Pat was a 28-year-old legal secretary. She was engaged to Tom, a 30-year-old factory supervisor. The couple had been living together for the past nine months. Their wedding had been planned for more than one year and included a church service and reception to which 100 guests were invited. Two weeks before the wedding, Tom called Pat's father, Bob, wondering if she was at her parents' house since she had not been home for the past two days.

Bob became concerned for his daughter when he learned from Tom that Pat had disappeared like this on three previous occasions. Tom told his future father-in-law that Pat had a problem with crack cocaine and that her earlier disappearances were due to her drug use. Bob called a treatment facility which had a community reputation for doing Interventions. The Invitational Interventionist followed the ARISE First Call procedures, with the goal of providing options for the family so they could decide the type and intensity of pressure needed to get Pat into treatment.

After the initial telephone coaching, Bob agreed to confer with Tom and the rest of the family about the next Intervention step. The following day Bob called the ARISE Interventionist back indicating that the family had decided to postpone the wedding and wanted to set up an appointment for an Intervention meeting where Pat would be approached and supported in getting into treatment.

The Intervention Network included Pat's father, Bob, who took on the role as Concerned Other/Family Link, her husband, Tom, and her brother, grandmother, and two aunts. The Interventionist developed a strategy with Bob that they appoint the paternal grandmother to be the key person to invite Pat to the intervention session. Despite Pat's anger, denial and initial refusal to come to the session, this approach proved successful. When the grandmother told her that the family was going to meet regardless of whether she came, Pat grasped the seriousness of her situation, and the commitment of her family to take whatever action was needed to help her get started in treatment.

This case demonstrates the ability of the family to do much of the Intervention preparation work on their own, mobilize the Intervention Network from a position of openness and inclusiveness, and ultimately show respect and caring for Pat by putting a decisive and quick plan of action together to intervene in her drug problem. One of the keys to success in this case was that instead of hiding Pat's crack problem from the rest of the family, Bob, Tom, and the Interventionist included them as resources, showing respect for them and for Pat.

ARISE Assumption 2. Intervention is a process, not an event.

Families commonly differ from each other in the ways they cope with addiction. There is a difference between a family with addiction and "an addicted family." The ARISE Invitational Intervention avoids the limitation of a "one size fits all" approach by offering a range of options designed for this particular situation by the Intervention Network, with the help of the ARISE Interventionist, to empower the family to recognize and use its unique strengths. The very nature of having options to choose from stimulates a new level of discussion about addiction.

The process of the Intervention Continuum not only encourages family members to take into account what *they* believe will work, but also persuades more families to start the Invitational Intervention process for their own benefit, not only on behalf of the AI. This dynamic occurs because in the First Call, the Interventionist is able to stress with the CO that the family will benefit, regardless of whether or not the AI attends any of the sessions.

A systemic view of addiction introduces the notion that the family is both affected by the problem and affects the course of the addiction. In addition to this interactive feedback loop, Invitational Intervention is designed to stop at the point where the AI enters treatment, which coincides with expenditure of the least effort possible.

Looking at Intervention as a process also takes into account what is known about changing behavior or habits. For instance, research related to smoking cessation has shown that an individual will attempt to stop between seven to nine times before being successful. Applying this information to Intervention would mean that it is important for the encouragement and support of the Intervention Network to take place over a period of time, through a number of difficulties and through the motivational challenges the AI will encounter in the process of change.

The Invitational Intervention is designed to work with the AI and the support network over the long term. Once the AI is engaged in treatment, the ARISE Intervention Network continues to meet to support the recovery process. The authors also believe that looking at Intervention as a process prepares the AI and family for the process of recovery by breaking from the addicted mindset of instant gratification and getting "what I want when I want it."

ARISE Assumption 3. Flexible Options (Regarding Level of Treatment, Willingness to Negotiate, and Working with the AI to Collaboratively Problem Solve) Maximize Potency and Minimize Resistance from Both the Intervention Network and Addicted Individual.

Families have multi-dimensional and complex relationships with the AI. Their loved one with the problem was not always an addict. Prior to the development of the addiction, the family had made a significant investment in him/her. Families often talk about how they have *lost* their loved one to addiction, and how they don't even know him/her anymore because of the serious changes in behavior, attitude, and over-all functioning. By the time the addiction has progressed to the point of undertaking an Intervention, the family has become desperate and does not believe there are any options for them other than requesting professional help.

Partnering with the family and using a flexible model that empowers and includes their ideas and goals, encourages the family to work from its own strengths. This approach also takes into account the dynamic that family relationships are complex and are rarely defined along the singular dimension of addictive disease. Encouraging the family to approach the AI with a selection of choices minimizes the likelihood of evoking a rebellious response in reaction to being told what to do. Often the AI agrees to attend the first meeting, "as long as you know I am coming to *only one* meeting." Invitational Intervention accepts whatever option works for the family and the AI.

ARISE Assumption 4. Pressure from the Intervention Network Needs to Match the Intensity of Resistance from the AI.

The goal of ARISE is to apply the least amount of pressure and energy by both family and Invitational Interventionist to motivate the AI to engage in treatment. The availability of options, beginning with an invitation, allows the family to decide what degree of pressure is needed to engage the AI in treatment. This approach has its parallel in medicine, where one applies the least invasive procedure to accomplish the goal.

Most families readily understand and appreciate this gradual escalation of pressure and are willing to increase pressure as long as it is done in a logical and sequential fashion. This gradual increase allows the family to set progressively tougher consequences, matching the level of pressure to the AI's reaction to the previous pressure.

Case Example
Sibling Intervenes with a Sibling

This case demonstrates the use of a sibling as the CO/Family Link in contending with a reluctant parent and how to deal with a family who wants to do a Johnson style Intervention. In this case, the AI entered treatment after just two weeks—drastic measures were not needed, and confrontation would have most likely caused the individual to withdraw from his family and their demands.

Sam was a 24-year-old construction laborer and the youngest of five children. Sam had previous legal problems related to drug and alcohol use, including unlawful possession of cocaine, DWI and resisting arrest. What precipitated the First Call was that Sam had borrowed his brother's car the night before, and had been involved in an accident after leaving a bar. His oldest brother, a psychiatric nurse, called the outpatient treatment facility to set up an Intervention. He had read about Johnson Interventions and wanted to undertake this style of Intervention with his brother.

The ARISE Intervention sequence was explained to the oldest brother and, although skeptical, he agreed to discuss it with the rest of the family and call back with a decision. The biggest differences between the ARISE Intervention and the Johnson Intervention in this case were: avoiding the elements of surprise, harsh confrontation, and severe consequences. The ARISE model included Sam in the negotiations concerning his level of care, and preparation sessions prior to the Intervention meeting were not necessary.

After discussing Invitational Intervention with the family, the oldest brother called back indicating the family was willing to use the ARISE method as long as there was no negotiating around level of care: The family was insistent that inpatient rehabilitation be used as a starting point with Sam because of his mother's worry about Sam's depression and potential suicide.

The family invited Sam to the intervention session, explained their concerns, had a discussion with him about the chemical dependency problem, and insisted he go to an inpatient program. He complied within two weeks. During the next two weeks, the family met twice on their own and started attending Al-Anon, fully preparing themselves for the possibility that Sam might choose to continue his drug use and refuse treatment.

The family members had never been this open and able to communicate with one another before and they were now able to support each other in a new way. The family also was able to continuously convey their Recovery Message (Chapter 1) to Sam while waiting for his decision. They reported less fear and more "peace of mind" knowing they were working in unison to solve an identified problem.

ARISE Assumption 5. Families Care about the Addicted Individual and the Addicted Individual Cares About the Family.

The very nature of a family's making the effort to learn about an Intervention exemplifies their concern and love for an addicted individual. As cited in Chapter 1, research on connectedness demonstrates that AIs have continuous contact with their families, despite the problems associated with the disease. Reviews of the literature on the regularity of family-of-origin contact conclude that 60-80% of drug abusers either live with their parents or are in daily face-to-face contact or telephone contact with at least one parent. Family patterns of loyalty, power dynamics and hierarchies, boundaries, communication, life-long investment, intergenerational dynamics and protectiveness make families more "powerful" than interventionists to effect change.

Case Example
Parent Intervenes With an Adolescent

This example underscores the relative ease of getting adolescents into treatment. Most Intervention calls about adolescents come as the result of problem behavior in school or at home, difficulty with the legal system, or the discovery of drug use. There are a number of similarities between The ARISE Intervention and José Szapocznik's Structural-Strategic Systems Engagement (SSSE), a highly successful and empirically proven method of Intervention with adolescents that achieves a treatment engagement rate of 92%.

Tracy was a 16-year-old whose primary residence was with her biological mother. While she was at her father's home for the weekend, he found small clear plastic bags of cannabis ("nickel bags") in her coat pocket. He called his ex-wife to let her know he had found the drugs. He reported that the ensuing discussion "opened my eyes to what was going on right under my nose." For the first time, he could make sense of Tracy's drop in grades at school, her defiant attitude, and her change of friends.

Because Tracy had no prior history of problem behavior, and was in advanced courses at school, he had previously thought the changes he was seeing reflected a "phase my daughter was going through." The parents decided to confront Tracy about finding the drugs and set up an appointment for a substance abuse evaluation. Tracy attended the evaluation session with her parents, and when confronted with the evidence of her substance abuse and behavior changes, agreed to begin outpatient treatment and attend Narcotics Anonymous.

Tracy reported in subsequent network sessions that one of the major motivating factors in her agreeing to seek treatment was the guilt and sadness she felt at hearing the pain she had caused her parents. She had violated their trust and violated the very values taught in her childhood. Their caring for her parents was a strong motivating factor in her seeking help.

ARISE Assumption 6. Working With Family Strengths Conveys a Belief That Family Resilience Can Overcome Obstacles.

Every family considering an Intervention has functioned as a family before the contact with an Interventionist and will continue to function once the contact is completed. The goal of ARISE is to elicit and use the inherent family strengths by encouraging the family members to do as much of the work as possible, with minimal involvement by the Interventionist. The approach is designed to guide families to recognize and apply their strengths toward stopping the destructive path of the addiction. The Invitational Intervention method trusts in the inherent competence of families and the ability of families to heal themselves, given the trust, encouragement, resources and guidance to do so.

Case Example
Spouse Intervenes with a Spouse

What makes this case interesting is that expanding the network provided enough support for the referring spouse to stand firm in her ultimatum, demanding her husband start on the path towards recovery. She backed off from a divorce that would have left her isolated and possibly alienated from her children. The case also demonstrates the flexibility of the ARISE model, showing how the intervention sequence may be used even when the initial request is not for an Intervention.

Peggy was a 40-year-old real estate sales agent. She had been married to Roger, a store manager, for 18 years. The couple had two teenage daughters, aged 13 and 15. Roger had a 15-year history of alcoholism and a two-year history of using powder cocaine. Peggy had recently called the police to the house after Roger became violent. The police took Roger to the hospital because of a hand laceration caused by his punching a hole in the wall. Following his release from the hospital, and at the suggestion of the police, Roger went to a motel room. Peggy called the outpatient treatment facility for help with her children who had witnessed the violence and were emotionally distraught and confused.

When Peggy and her daughters met with an ARISE Invitational Interventionist for the first time, one of the sources of conflict in the home became clear—the children were very upset about their mother's threat to separate from their father. They thought their mother provoked much of the violence by her screaming and threatening remarks. Peggy admitted that her resentment and anger toward Roger often surfaced with her losing her temper in front of the children.

The ARISE Interventionist met with Peggy alone and explained the ARISE Invitational Intervention sequence to her. During the ensuing discussion, Peggy talked about her love for Roger, how he had changed over the past couple of years, her resulting mistrust of him, and how the major source of her anger was their current financial problems. She agreed to keep Roger out of the house until an ARISE Intervention network meeting was held.

Peggy saw the upcoming ARISE meeting as a last chance for Roger to either get into treatment or experience the consequences of a separation. She believed a network meeting would help her follow through with a separation because, after a thorough discussion with a professional present, she thought that the Intervention Network would support her decision to separate and she would feel less guilt. She wanted to invite Roger's mother (his father was deceased), both of her parents, the children, Roger's brother and his wife, and his employer to the Intervention meeting. The primary purpose of the session was to confront Roger on his addiction and to support Peggy in setting consequences if he continued to use.

However, with the combined support of the extended family, Peggy was able to realize how many strengths and resources they had to be able to work through this problem, and Roger was able to start treatment for his addiction and keep his family together.

ARISE Assumption 7. The Intervention Network Benefits from the Process Regardless of Whether the Addicted Individual Enters Treatment.

Most other Intervention models are not designed to provide ongoing support to other members of the Intervention Network after the Intervention ends. Research by Barber and Gilbertson shows that subjective reporting by family members regarding family relationships and marital functioning is no better one year after a successful Intervention. In contrast to other forms of Intervention, *Invitational* Intervention has the dual focus of engaging the AI in treatment *and* supporting the family members in healing from the effects of living with addiction. It is directed toward both individual *and* family recovery. It is designed to work with the family whether or not the AI enters treatment as Invitational Intervention is designed as a process—not merely a one-time event.

Case Example
Adult Child Intervenes with a Parent

Ted was a 55-year-old man with a 25-year history of chronic alcoholism. He had not worked for the past seven years since being laid off from his factory job when the plant closed. He had been on medical disability for the past four years after injuring his back in an alcohol-related fall. Ted was divorced and lived alone in an apartment with his oldest daughter Tammy living in the flat above him. He had two other daughters and a son. (One of these daughters had achieved a year of recovery from her alcoholism.)

Ted had been through more than ten hospitalizations for detoxification and had failed to complete numerous inpatient and outpatient treatment programs successfully. He had cirrhosis of the liver, peripheral neuropathy, and symptoms of organic brain damage. The ARISE Interventionist received a call from his daughter who wanted to do an Intervention with her father. Tammy indicated that he had been taken to the hospital emergency department the previous day after falling on the sidewalk and was unable to stand up. Ted was admitted to the detoxification unit with a .32 Blood Alcohol Content.

The Interventionist described the three Levels of ARISE and suggested that the family come to a Level I session while her father was in the hospital so that they could discuss possible options. Tammy was instructed to tell her father that this family meeting was taking place. The meeting included all four children and Ted's two older sisters. The first ARISE Intervention session reviewed how sick Ted was. The Interventionist stressed that there was a strong likelihood that Ted might die from his continued drinking. Family issues of loss, anger, mistrust and sadness were acknowledged.

The aims of the first Intervention session were to (a) get a commitment from the family to continue sessions so they could support each other if Ted continued to drink, and (b) have a plan of action to stop his alcohol abuse, which would include options and consequences to be conveyed to him in the hospital. The family immediately saw the value of continued ARISE sessions. They decided they would prefer not to allow Ted to return to his apartment, and insisted that he either go to a long-term residential treatment program or live with one of his older sisters for a minimum of six months. He was also to participate in outpatient treatment and be active in Alcoholics Anonymous before being allowed to move back into his own apartment.

The family met with Ted in the hospital to convey their concerns and strong recommendations. The family understood that ultimately the choice was Ted's and that he might reject their love, support, and their plan. Initially, Ted fought his family, wanting to return to his apartment. The family's insistence, their united approach, and their openness about their intention to continue their family recovery, even if he chose to reject their plan (they would then be preparing for his death), convinced Ted of the seriousness of the situation. Having two options in the plan allowed Ted to save face by holding onto his authority and autonomy while negotiating with his family which plan he would choose. He chose to go to his sister's house and to start attending an outpatient alcoholism treatment that included weekly sessions with his family.

This example demonstrates the potential pressure that adult children can exert with chemically dependent parents. Health problems are often a powerful motivator for starting recovery, and in this situation, the natural progression of problems that develop from untreated addiction was used as a primary motivator. In addition, this example illustrates how an Invitational Intervention method offers help for family members even if the addicted individual does not stop using. The Invitational Intervention process would still have strengthened the family's overall functioning and connectedness with one another, even if Ted had not stopped using,

The goal of all Intervention methods is to get the AI into treatment.

No one Intervention method can address all situations. Hopefully, the awareness of differences in methods will result in more AIs getting the treatment they need to recover from addiction because the Intervention method will be matched to the situational needs and/or circumstances of the family and the AI. The authors believe this is an area—matching Intervention method to family needs, history, and current situation—that needs further research and could result in more families using an Intervention.

The following table is designed to summarize for the reader a point-by-point comparison of Invitational Intervention functions and Johnson Intervention functions using the above noted ARISE assumptions. In operational terms, the table clarifies how a Johnson Interventionist would approach a situation compared with how an ARISE Interventionist would respond in that same situation. The table is meant to stimulate discussion and awareness of the differences in Intervention methods and the implications of those differences, for Interventionists, families and the AI.

INTERVENTION PREMISES: A COMPARISON OF THE JOHNSON AND ARISE INTERVENTIONS	
ARISE Intervention	**Johnson Intervention**
ARISE Assumption 1. Involving the Addicted Individual (AI) in the Intervention process from the beginning conveys respect and encourages openness within the system.	
Continuity of contact, open discussion without secrecy, and respect for the AI as a person, all reduce the need for surprise.	The AI is caught by surprise with defenses down, increasing the likelihood of treatment entry.
Network's respect for AI's ambivalence toward entering the recovery process matches the level of pressure with AI's resistance.	The maximum level of confrontation is assumed to be needed for all AIs.
ARISE Assumption 2. Intervention is a process not an event.	
Motivation to Change is a process not an event.	One-time confrontation is the impetus for change.
Intervention Continuum is tailored to AI's behavior.	Programmed Intervention proceeds regardless of the AI's behaviors.
The transition from a focus on treatment engagement to support for recovery is one of several objectives.	The engagement of the AI in treatment is the only goal.
Support for recovery is the final option on a continuum.	Engagement in treatment is the first and only option.
ARISE Assumption 3. Flexible options maximize potency and minimize resistance from network and AI.	
Negotiation process is encouraged.	Network avoids negotiation to reduce AI's manipulative power.
Flexible options provide choices during extended ARISE process reducing fear of proceeding.	Options are limited by a one-time intervention.
ARISE Assumption 4. Pressure from the intervention network needs to match the intensity of resistance from the AI.	
Level and type of pressure are sequenced in response to AI's resistance.	Singular event combines confrontation and invariable consequences.
Consequences are designed to match AI's resistance over time until AI enters treatment.	There is a one-time intervention, therefore, one set of consequences.

ARISE Assumption 5. Families care about the AI, and AIs care about their families.	
Negotiation builds on Network's past trust, accountability and involvement with AI.	Network's mistrust of AI results in avoidance of negotiation.
Sequential process and ongoing monitoring make future Intervention possible if this one fails.	Process ends with the Intervention whether it succeeds or fails.
ARISE Assumption 6. Working from family strengths conveys a belief that family resilience can overcome obstacles.	
Outpatient treatment is preferred to maximize continued network involvement.	The usual aim is the AI's entry into inpatient treatment.
Network strengths are elicited to maintain support for AI throughout the process.	Letters to AI convey only initial love and support.
ARISE Assumption 7. The intervention network benefits from the process whether or not the AI enters treatment.	
The network builds support and self care.	Network relationships and self-care are not addressed.
Shared stories, strengthened relationships and support result in systemic change, often breaking an intergenerational cycle. The aim is both individual and family recovery.	Systemic change is not relevant to the singular event of the Intervention. The aim is individual treatment entry.
Parallel goals of getting the AI into treatment and building positive relationships between the AI and the network are addressed, ensuring better network function regardless of the AI's actions.	Ongoing functioning of the network is not a primary concern.

The following points summarize the authors' responses to the question: *Why use an ARISE Invitational Intervention?*

ARISE:
- Is a collaborative process. From the initial invitation extended, the process conveys respect and establishes the ground rules for openness and no secrecy from the very beginning
- Acknowledges that mistrust will be a major issue and assures the addicted individual that s/he can trust family/ friends and does not have to trust the Interventionist
- Allows the Interventionist to say, "We will all meet for the first time together," and "Let the addicted person know s/he is only being asked to come to this one meeting."

- It addresses the addicted individual's biggest complaint, fear, and source of defensiveness—"I'm being tricked," "You're going behind my back," or "You're ambushing me and doing this as a surprise."
- Views the First Caller/Concerned Other as a valuable necessary resource in getting the AI into treatment, rather than viewing him/her as co-dependent or enabling.
- Encourages the Intervention Network to make a solid commitment to the process, even if the AI refuses to come to the First Meeting
- Acknowledges the power and destructiveness of addiction and recognizes how the addicted individual needs support & encouragement to begin a process of recovery
- Breaks the isolation and "private struggle" of both AI and family
- Sets the groundwork for the Intervention Network to be used as a "Board of Directors" for consensus decision making
- Establishes roles and clarification of the process and asserts the initial rule that the group is going to meet regardless of whether the addicted individual attends meetings
- Empowers the family, builds on family competence, resilience and strengths, offering hope and reducing blame, shame and guilt
- Acknowledges boundaries for the family, the Intervention Network, and the AI
- Sets the scene for the initial and future meetings——the Invitational Intervention Continuum
- Acknowledges the importance of choice at every step in the Intervention
- Offers the AI options, and thereby avoids the rebellious/ defiant response set up by telling him/her what to do
- Removes the power of the addictive disease from controlling and defining the family

CHAPTER 3
Family Motivation to Change: Part I Operational Principles and Background

What is Family Motivation to Change?

Family Motivation to Change can best be understood as the combined forces operating within a family guiding it toward maintaining survival and healthy functioning in the face of serious threat, and toward healing when that threat is removed. The authors discovered that the force driving a family toward health is the same force that in other families, generations before, drove them to the initial adaptive behavior where a family member becomes addicted in an attempt to keep the family close, divert them from their anxiety, arguments and concerns, and prevent them from feeling the pain of intense loss and sorrow by redirecting their focus. The concept, "Family Motivation to Change," is based on the belief in the inherent competence and resilience of families.

The authors have worked extensively with families following major disaster, social upheaval, untimely death or unexpected loss. This work, so close to the onset of trauma, sorrow and loss that frequently accompanies major tragedy, allowed the authors to step directly into the grief that initiates the problem of addiction.

Definition of Family

For our purposes, we define family as *"a domestic group of people, or a number of domestic groups, linked through descent (demonstrated or stipulated) from a common ancestor, marriage, or other committed coupling, legal or informal adoption, or through the choice to become kin to each other. It includes the extended intergenerational family network, by blood or choice, in its broadest sense."*

It is difficult to conceive of a culture surviving without the family. Families are the core unit of social relationships across all cultures. "The family is the natural context for both growth and healing. It is the natural group that over time has evolved patterns of interacting. These patterns make up the family structure, which governs the functioning of family members, delineating their range of behavior and facilitating their interaction. A viable form of family structure is needed to perform the family's essential tasks of supporting individuation while providing a sense of belonging" (Minuchin & Fishman, 1981, page 112).

This understanding of family allows clinicians to work with Concerned Others (COs) to recognize that this reaching out to help a loved one is healthy, rather than viewing it as co-dependent or enabling. True, the CO and others who come together as the Intervention Network in support of the individual with an addiction may need to examine their behaviors as the process of change evolves. However, the initial reaching out, by the First Caller, must be viewed positively. It must also be responded to at the level of the request—in other words, beginning where the family is, not where we as clinicians, or as a treatment system, expect them to be.

Impact of Stressors/Change on Family Functioning

While change is a natural part of living, experiencing multiple transitions, typically three or more (even normal, predictable life-cycle events such as the birth of a baby, promotion of a breadwinner, or the death of an elder), within a short period of time, can create stress in a family. Stressors, such as premature death, massive or unpredictable loss, cultural conflict, and unresolved grief result in families being thrown off track from their usual healthy functioning. During such times, the Transitional Pathway—the fragile but essential line, the psychological and emotional sense of connection between individuals' and families' past, present and future—can easily become disrupted. If disrupted, an asynchrony between the rate and direction with which individual family members adjust to change results in what is termed a "transitional conflict."

In such situations, individual family members become symptomatic and develop adaptive behaviors (without conscious intent) that are initially designed to protect the family from pain, keep families close, and help rebuild homeostatic functioning. At times of overwhelming grief, families find ways of compensating and staying close together. Frequently, one member of the family will begin to use alcohol or other substances, or exhibit other symptoms that serve the dual purpose of drawing the family's attention away from the grief and holding the family together to deal with the problems arising from the new problem behavior or symptoms.

The result is that the family is unable to process all of the current transitions, remaining locked in the transitional conflict of the moment. Family members then become focused on the symptomatic member rather than on the more painful trauma. As the family maintains its closeness, grief is assuaged and the original pain is reduced. When the symptoms or alcohol/drug use are reduced, the pain and grief return, reinforcing the need for the problem. An addiction cycle is set, and often transmitted across generations until the family grieving is resolved and the symptom has become redundant; only then can healing occur.

Viewed in this context, the onset of addiction, as a form of adaptive behavior, developed initially as an attempt to protect the family. However, over time, and through generations, this symptomatic behavior no longer served to protect the family. The pattern that had developed was transmitted simply as a way of being—something the family simply accepted as normal—an intergenerational pattern that now, rather than being highly adaptive and functional, had become dysfunctional or even destructive.

These patterns that are transmitted across generations, ultimately preventing the family from progressing from one family life cycle stage to the next, are transmitted unintentionally and with no awareness of their origin, or that they were grounded in an initial attempt to protect the family from pain. Often we refer to families like this who are seeking help as being "stuck." Other "symptomatic" behaviors include: depression, suicidality, post-traumatic stress, sexual risk-taking and violence.

A look at the impact of genocide, such as the Holocaust, or the recent Balkan war, and the onset of addiction in subsequent generations from previously abstemious cultures, vividly demonstrates this point. For example, studies of Jewish holocaust survivor families provide a staggering demonstration of how alcoholism results from disruption of family connectedness, family continuity and cultural transition. The rate of alcoholism in Jewish families prior to World War II was extremely low, while research after World War II shows alcoholism rates in subsequent generations of Jewish families that approach those in the population at large. This increase relates to the disruption in traditional family functioning, forced migration, conflicts in cultural transition and the significant number of holocaust related deaths.

Another example is that seen in refugee populations where addiction rates are approximately 30% higher than in the general population. The same problem arises after major disaster. For example, within one year after September 11, 2001, there was a 31% increase in the rate of substance abuse and addiction in New York City and its immediate surroundings—approximating the addiction statistics of uprooted persons around the world.

We believe that if increased family stressors and unresolved transitional conflict are related to the development of symptomatic behavior in individual family members, then a decrease in stressors and resolution of transitional conflict is likely to result in the return of competent family functioning and healthier individual functioning.

Our goal in the ARISE process is to empower families to identify their inherent resilience and the resources that they can successfully use to address the problem with addiction that confronts them. This guiding principle forms the basis of "Family Motivation to Change," and the process of Invitational Intervention to help families get a resistant addicted loved one into treatment.

Family Resilience

Often, clinicians are overwhelmed by the complexity and seemingly endless pattern of destructive behaviors caused by addiction with which families present. This is understandable when addiction is viewed in isolation from the family system and from its initial adaptive function. ARISE is a method that, from the first phone call, helps families access their strengths and resilience. The family seeking help has survived and prevailed for generations, functioning and supportive (albeit at times often limping along), despite multiple assaults and traumas,

When people are able to access their past resilience by being in touch with their history and reconnecting the disrupted transitional pathway, they can then understand that their family's intergenerational history of addiction might well have been started as an attempt at adapting to significant loss. They begin to trace the pattern of attempted protection from pain, and can see how the symptomatic behavior and the subsequent multigenerational addictive disease served to keep the family together until their grief had been resolved.

This knowledge frees the current generation from their overwhelming sense of guilt, shame, blame, and the inevitability of a future locked into addiction. Hope is reignited. A paradigm shift has occurred, not only for the clients or patients, but for their clinicians as well. This shift in itself allows the entire Intervention Network to move forward in the process with new vigor.

The authors have found it important to understand the difference between a "family with addiction" and "an addicted family." The former enters the process with a firm belief that change is attainable: the latter may feel inescapably stuck in an immutable pattern that relentlessly transmits laterally and vertically across the family genogram. A family with addiction (often a family without an inter-generational pattern of addiction) will move through an Invitational Intervention with purpose, commitment and relatively quick success. An addicted family (one whose interaction, rituals, and connectedness revolve around addictive behaviors that have evolved through multiple generations) will often present with more ambivalence, more internal disagreement/conflict, more blaming behaviors, more fears, and thus require more time to complete the Invitational Intervention process.

It is important to understand that whether working with a family with addiction or with an addicted family, both have strengths and resilience to draw on. The ARISE strategies used with each family may differ, but the underlying belief in family competence and resilience will always remain the same. The approaches for both situations are addressed in Chapters 8 and 9.

One strategy that ARISE uses to emphasize the inclusiveness of the Invitational Intervention process is to develop a Recovery Message that is given to the AI as part of the invitation to attend the first meeting (see Chapter 6). This Recovery Message is typically built around the reconnection of the family transitional pathway, explicitly stating the understanding of where the addiction in the family started (where it came from), and the intent to stop the addiction from progressing into future generations (where the family is now). This is a crucial idea to convey to the AI because it shows that the family does not blame him/her, that they recognize the entire family's need to heal, and that the individual is not expected to do this alone.

Applying this Recovery Message allows both the Intervention

Network and the AI to recognize and use biological, psychological, social, and spiritual resources in making informed choices about what cherished ideas and beliefs to keep from their past, which to draw on for the future, and what to leave behind as no longer being necessary. Deep strength, motivation, and hope come from connecting the past with the future through the present.

Family Connectedness

The acknowledgement that families have a vested interest in their members is particularly relevant for practitioners dealing with addiction because a prevailing belief in the field is that individuals struggling with recovery from addiction should be kept at a distance from their families. Counter to this notion, the ARISE method builds on the connectedness of, and works with, families to explore how to access and maintain resilience and competence across time in order to break the inter-generational transmission of addiction.

The connection of the addict to his/her family of origin is well documented. In fact, contrary to the common perception in the field, addicts care about their families and their families care about them. They remain very closely connected; in fact, more closely connected than the general population. When the initial adaptive functioning of addiction is considered, it follows that AIs would maintain closeness to their families and vice versa. Averaging several studies, approximately 9% of non-addicts tend to call their families daily, while AIs maintain daily contact with their families at a rate of approximately 57% in the US, 62% in England, 80% in Thailand and Italy, and 67% in Puerto Rico. These cross-cultural examples of connectedness demonstrate empirically that this dynamic plays out in families across the world.

ARISE builds on the strength and function of this connectedness. The CO has become aware (either consciously or subconsciously) that the protective function of addiction is no longer needed. S/he now knows that the AI cannot get into recovery without help because of the inherent nature of the disease of addiction—a disease that "tells" the AI that s/he doesn't even have a disease.

Individual Motivation to Change

ARISE harnesses these close family ties and the family's motivation to help the addicted member rather than relying only on the individual's motivation, which is often shaky and ambivalent at best. The recognition that the family is a key factor is especially important with addiction, demonstrated how few individuals ever get into recovery entirely on their own. The Invitational Intervention method puts into operational terms the recovery slogan that most addicts get into recovery as the result of "a nudge, with a grudge or from a judge."

Prochaska and DiClemente's Stages of Change model represents six individual motivational stages that explain how an individual progresses from preparing for change to eventually taking action to change addictive behaviors and move into long-term recovery. The ARISE method focuses on how to harness the power and commitment of Family Motivation to Change with the goal of getting a resistant addict through these stages and into treatment.

Six Stages of Change:

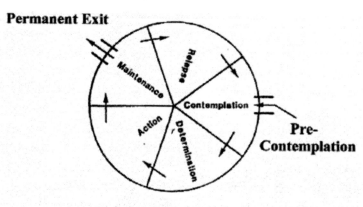

Prochaska and DiClemente's six stages of change.

The authors have learned that Family Motivation to Change positively influences all six of the Stages of Change. This chapter, however, will discuss only the first two stages of Prochaska and DiClimente's Individual Motivation to Change, because these are the two stages primarily impacted by Family Motivation to Change with regard to resistant addicts entering treatment.

In the first stage, Pre-Contemplation, the individual is typically too unwilling, unknowing, or unable to acknowledge that the substance abuse problem requires a change in behavior, attitude, friends, and drug/alcohol use. The AI in Pre-Contemplation, might believe that "No-one knows there is a problem," and that, "my using doesn't affect anyone else. It isn't hurting anyone but me—they could just leave me alone.".

Both beliefs are challenged—whether or not s/he actually attends—by mobilizing an Intervention Network and inviting the AI to attend the first meeting (using the Recovery Message developed from the First Call). The AI is forced to acknowledge the reality of the situation. Even if s/he refuses the invitation to attend any meetings, and the Intervention Network continues without his/her presence, the strength and resilience of the family is acknowledged and conveyed through continued contact with the AI. This continuity communicates the seriousness of the problem, and the unwavering commitment of the Intervention Network to support change.

Contemplation, the second stage, occurs when the AI is able to recognize that there is a substance abuse problem, which may require a change in behavior, attitude, friends and drug/alcohol use, but s/he is not yet ready to take action, or believes that "half measures" will be sufficient to solve the problem. During this stage, the AI may be trying any number of self-prescribed remedies. For instance, s/he may try to strike a bargain and offer "to go halfway," and "try to cut back" on the amount of drugs and alcohol used," stop using a specific drug, or go on a "marijuana maintenance" program to help stop drinking. Knowing, as we do, the chronic nature of addiction, these self-prescribed half measures will not work for long.

These two stages are marked by denial of the problem, resistance to getting help, and significant ambivalence. It is at these initial stages that Invitational Intervention operates to motivate resistant addicts to enter treatment. Imagine if you will, the addicted person presenting such remedies to an Intervention Network composed of family and close friends. Imagine even further, that the Intervention Network agrees to support the AI in his/her efforts to change, with the proviso that if these self-prescribed efforts do not work, s/he will agree to enter a treatment program. In this process, the AI builds his/her own motivation through testing and measuring the results.

The ARISE method turns the tables on negotiations with the AI and uses time to its maximum advantage because, having made an agreement with known consequences, s/he now owes accountability to the whole Intervention Network. Each time the group meets; the AI is asked about the success of the self-prescribed remedy.

This process of "self discovery" is not completely unlike the situation in the Big Book of Alcoholics Anonymous where the suggestion is made to the individual who is not convinced of the problem to continue drinking no more than two or three drinks at any one time for a period of 30 days. By the end of such a test period, most AIs will know the answer to their question about whether or not they are addicts. One advantage of ARISE is that the Intervention Network builds in the proviso for treatment if the self-remedies fail, as they inevitably will, due to the predictable and chronic nature of addiction.

CHAPTER 4
Family Motivation to Change: Part II The Process in Action

Operational Process

This chapter addresses a number of the operational components that explain how Family Motivation to Change works to get a loved one into addiction treatment. The Invitational Intervention process is typically activated by one member of the family, the First Caller serving as Family Link/Concerned Other (CO), who has the interest, motivation, strength, credibility and cross-generational knowledge of the family to act as a Family Link, and who is willing to coordinate the process. The key operational elements discussed below operate on both conscious and sub-conscious levels with the CO and the entire Intervention Network. Think of these techniques as the motivational gas that powers the family engine to operate productively and with maximum efficiency.

First Protecting and then Healing the Family

As discussed in Chapters 1 and 3, the initial protection of the family starts sub-consciously as one member of the family is drawn to offer him/herself through addiction as the sacrifice to serve as the diversion for a suffering loved one, and for the greater good of the family by helping them avoid the acute pain, sorrow and grief associated with this suffering. This driving force to survive—Family Motivation to Change—serves to prevent the loved ones and larger extended family from prolonged suffering, binding them together across generations until the grieving is resolved.

Each time that the AI starts to succeed at a job, a marriage, becoming a parent, or any other life cycle transition, his/her sacrificial diversion no longer stands as protection from suffering for his/her loved ones, and without the intensity of both the feelings and the activities needed to take care of him/her in the crisis, their feelings of depression, grief, or an overwhelming sense of loss is likely to return. At this point, there is a high probability that the AI will relapse in an attempt to save the loved ones yet again. Only when the original grief and transitional conflict are resolved throughout the extended family will the AI be free to succeed in making the life cycle transition and move solidly into long-term recovery.

At some [generally sub-conscious] level, the CO understands the self-sacrificial dynamic underlying the unacceptable, often self-destructive and disruptive behavior of the AI, and reaches out to initiate change. At the moment of the First Call, this initial motivation to protect the family becomes the driving force behind Family Motivation to Change. This First Call serves to challenge the family's need for self-sacrificial protection. By requesting help, rather than replicating the intergenerational pattern of the past, the Family Link is providing an opportunity for a major shift and the potential for long-term recovery of both AI and extended family.

Continued, unresolved grief results in addiction being transmitted across and down the generations until the grief is finally resolved, and one family member alone, serving as the CO/Family Link, can take responsibility for leading the family into healing. A key motivator for change is the understanding and acknowledgment that the initial protective function of symptomatic behaviors allows the addiction to become embedded in the family functioning throughout intergenerational transmission. This is an especially important concept to emphasize when there are young family members and the family realizes the high risk of addiction that can potentially be passed down to them. (Of course, addiction is also transmitted laterally across the family genogram.)

Any member of the family can start the process of breaking this intergenerational cycle of addiction. This can happen in a number of ways. It might be that an AI decides him/herself that this process needs to end. Or another concerned family member decides that this addictive disease will not take any more members of the family. The concerned family members are acting out of their commitment and motivation to stop the cycle of addiction from continuing into the next generation and are not necessarily consciously aware of the underlying factors of unresolved grief that play a fundamental role in the addiction process.

Completing the Transitional Task for "Peace of Mind."

As people approach vulnerable times in their lives, and are reminded of their mortality, either through aging, illness, or trauma, they begin to focus on what they want to accomplish before they die. For many, it might mean completing a life cycle transition such as leaving home, giving a daughter permission to marry, having a child, or completing the process of resolving grief. To quote an elderly patient, "I want peace of mind, heart, and soul before leaving this earth and facing my maker. I want to see my sons in recovery and know that my grandchildren will not also suffer the life of alcoholics as did my husband and my sons."

It is common for the CO to be an older parent calling about an adult child's addiction problem. The ARISE method offers hope for such families to stop the legacy of addiction and to allow parents to obtain their "peace of mind," knowing that their task of successful parenting has been completed. As one of our older parents commented after seeing his son go into recovery and rebuild a lost relationship with his children, "There is nothing better than a sober father being there for his children."

Getting a Loved One Back

Families usually observe significant changes in their addicted family member's behavior. They want to get their loved one back to what s/he was like before the alcohol and/or drug use started. They'll say, "It feels like I have lost my daughter," or "That is not my father any more; he was never like that until the drinking got worse."

What family members will describe is the memory of their loved one's functioning before addiction, and how the individual changed over time as the process of addiction became more and more intrusive; eventually changing thought patterns, attitudes, coping abilities and behaviors. The family wants their addicted loved one back the way s/he was before the addiction. This longing is a powerful motivator for change.

It is not an easy journey to get a loved one back, or for the AI to reclaim the trust of the family they have hurt due to their use of alcohol and/or drugs. However, families are resilient and competent, and possess tremendous resources that can be guided toward productive use. Once the process is initiated by a CO, the ARISE Interventionist has a significant opportunity to harness the family's motivation and resilience.

Preventing Further Loss

Families are acutely aware of the risk of losing their loved one due to the destructiveness of his/her acting out behaviors. The intense connectedness of family members, beginning with the first family member becoming addicted, may reflect the life cycle stage where the original loss or transitional conflict occurred. This transitional stage, or "stuck place," may actually prevent further loss by holding family members close together until the grieving is complete.

Family connectedness is a key dynamic that mobilizes family members to serve as effective Family Links between the professionals and the family, allowing clinicians to "coach" them and their addicted loved ones to enter treatment and continue in recovery. At the point of the First Call, the CO is making a tacit statement to the family to end the pattern of addiction. This emerging dynamic is Family Motivation to Change in action and is essential in the achievement of long-term growth and sustained change.

Case Example

The authors are currently consulting with the Kosova Ministry of Health and European Agency for Reconstruction (EAR) to assist in the design and implementation of the Addiction Education, Resource and Tertiary Treatment Center in Pristina, Kosova, and the development of country-wide addiction services for Kosova——the first addiction treatment system in that country. The following case example demonstrates Family Motivation to Change, highlighting the onset of the problem, what triggered the need for the distraction from pain, and providing a "real-world" example of the operational protocols in action.

Many of the cases coming into the Addictions Treatment Center are related to trauma and loss associated with the war and ethnic cleansing. Because there is little inter-generational history of addiction in the Kosovar families—the predominant culture is secular Islam—the situation presents a unique opportunity to witness how families get off track and how addiction develops as an adaptation to major trauma and loss, before being transmitted into future generations. The following case example demonstrates this process.

Sanja is a 17-year-old female living with her widowed 46-year-old father, Jusuf. The youngest of three children, she was 11 years old when the war broke out in Kosova. The family lived in Pristina, the capital of Kosova, and both parents were college educated. Her father worked as an engineer for an electrical plant and her mother was an elementary school teacher. The family valued education and placed a high expectation on completing college.

When the war broke out, the electrical power plant in which Sanja's father worked was destroyed. Sanja's mother was taken from their home and later found dead. Jusuf went into a serious depression after the death of his wife and subsequently experienced problems with depression, including an inability to work.

Up to the age of 15, Sanja was described as a talented student with a keen interest in mathematics and chemistry. Then she began to exhibit acting out behaviors that included the following: mood changes, skipping school, not doing homework, not coming home at night, defiance toward her father, sexual risk-taking, and changing her peer group to older youths known to be heavy drinkers and drug users. Jusuf did not understand the root of his daughter's defiant behavior and the result was increased arguing and fighting between them.

At one point, Sanja was hospitalized overnight for symptoms that resembled a drug overdose, but she vehemently denied any use of drugs at the time of this incident. When discharged from the hospital, Sanja was referred to a mental health outpatient service but refused to go. Sanja continued to exhibit out of control behaviors over the course of the next few months, consistently protesting that she did not drink alcohol or use drugs.

Jusuf, increasingly suspicious of his daughter's drug and alcohol use, called the Addictions Treatment Center to find out what he could do to get help for his daughter because she was refusing his attempts to get her treatment. Using the ARISE protocol, Jusuf was coached to approach his daughter with love rather than threats or anger, and to express his growing concern for her wellbeing.

He was instructed to let her know that he would not tolerate her continued acting out and that he had set up an appointment at a treatment facility and expected her to accompany him. He planned to tell her that he would be going to the session whether or not she decided to attend. By these actions, Jusuf was applying the driving force of Family Motivation to Change to get his resistant daughter Sanja started in treatment in an effort to establish a positive relationship with her and to prevent further loss.

In the first meeting, attended by Jusuf and his daughter Sanja, the genogram and timeline created together with the family and the ARISE Interventionist revealed that Jusuf and Sanja had suffered multiple losses. Not only had Jusuf lost his wife, and Sanja her mother, but Jusuf's mother (Sanja's grandmother) who had moved in with him to help with Sanja had also died. Sanja had, therefore, lost two key women in her life within one year. She had also witnessed her father falling into a depression, essentially losing him as well. In addition, Sanja had suffered the trauma of living in a war zone when she was only 11.

During the meeting, Sanja continued to deny any alcohol or drug use, in spite of her prior hospitalization for a suspected overdose. When Sanja was asked if she worried about her father, she softened, starting to cry. She spoke of the history of his depression and how she was constantly concerned about him. It was evident that she understood the impact of her father's loss on his ability to function.

From a family life cycle point of view, it is clear that Sanja was caught in a dilemma regarding the eventuality of her leaving home. Even though her becoming more independent would soon be natural and age appropriate, she realized that this action would affect her father with yet another loss, because she was all that he had left. Knowing that her leaving home would most likely increase her father's depression and, unable to express these thoughts and feelings, even to herself, Sanja had started acting out by using alcohol and drugs. She did this in an attempt to distract her father from his pain and depression. Jusuf unable to manage his daughter's defiance and acting out behaviors, was unaware that Sanja, in her own unconscious way, was trying to take care of him and his unresolved grief. His response was to kick Sonja out of their home. It might appear that Sanja's dilemma about leaving her father and the resulting loss would be resolved by her father's action of expelling her from their home. However, once the clinician shared her understanding and explained about the possible origin of her acting out behavior, Sanja was able to admit to her alcohol and drug use. Even though she did not fully understand the impact of her actions, she was able to see that the underlying reason for her behavior was in the hopes that he would want her out of the house. This would potentially minimize the feeling of guilt on her part, and a sense of abandonment on her father's.

Shortly after this meeting, Sanja agreed to stop her drug and alcohol use. The clinicians proceeded to: (a) help Jusuf see how much Sanja loved and was willing to sacrifice for him; (b) encourage Sanja to see that she did not have to sacrifice herself in order to leave home successfully; (c) ensure that Jusuf received treatment for depression; (d) work with father and daughter to address the "normal" loss of a child leaving home, and, at the same time, (e) plan for supporting a continuing relationship between the two, appropriate to the life cycle of the family.

Sanja's adaptive behaviors were designed to protect her father from experiencing another loss and increased depression, and to take his mind off the multiple losses and unresolved grief in the family. If unaddressed, one might project how this adaptive behavior could have resulted in her "pseudo-individuation" (getting kicked out of the house rather than leaving home successfully). The asynchrony of Sanja's readiness to leave home, her father's need for her to stay, and her sense that he needed her to salve his depression, demonstrates the classic foundation of a generic transitional conflict that may then be transmitted across generations. Had Sanja stayed to "save her father," this adaptive solution would likely have become the demonstrable pattern that future generations would have emulated.

The patterns that would have emerged had there *not* been an Intervention can be explored using this case as a foundational base, Without an Intervention, the unresolved losses and development of addiction would have caused perpetual acting out behaviors in future generations. For this family, the recurrent transitional conflicts first surfaced at the life cycle stage of leaving home. After a number of generations, when the transitional conflict is not resolved, the conflict would move to an earlier and earlier life cycle stage. In this case, Sanja's grandchildren might struggle with transitional conflict at puberty or adolescence and begin displaying symptomatic behavior at that time; Subsequent generations might have problems with separation anxiety and school refusal.

If Jusuf had died before these issues were resolved and while his daughter was still out of the house using alcohol and drugs, Sanja would likely feel intense guilt that her father had died alone and grieving. Her guilt would be exacerbated because she would believe "that she was not there for him when he really needed her." She would have felt responsible for making him suffer yet another loss, and her guilt would probably have resulted in her being unable to resolve her own grief over his death, therefore preventing her own successful passage through adult life cycles.

The saga of intergenerational unresolved grief for this family would have begun—first Jusuf, then his daughter. Sanja's grief and increased guilt over not being there for her father at the time of his dying would predictably result in her increasing alcohol and drug use, ensuring that she cross the line from abuse into addiction. This is a common story related by many addicts in recovery. They recount dramatically increased use associated with a significant death, followed shortly afterwards by crossing the line into compulsive behavior, whether through alcohol, drugs, sexual compulsion, gambling, or another addiction.

In the ARISE method, Family Motivation to Change is the primary factor that, in the context of resolving grief and loss, increases the likelihood of long-term recovery for the AI.

CHAPTER 5
Summary of ARISE Development, Background and Philosophy

Invitational Intervention, and the ARISE method, build on earlier Intervention models that evolved primarily from addictions theory or were individually focused (e.g., Johnson Intervention, Unilateral Interventions for Women, Unilateral Family Therapy). ARISE is rooted in concepts and methods developed within family and systems theory——particularly social network therapy, Transitional Family Therapy and the network approach to substance abuse treatment.

Other systemic influences on the ARISE method include: loyalty patterns in families; family hierarchy; family boundaries; inter-generational dynamics; ecosystemic theories; the larger systems approach, and the importance of rituals and story-telling. Although ARISE draws heavily from theories used in family and systems therapy, it is a pre-treatment engagement technique. It is not therapy. When clinicians use the ARISE method, their sole focus is getting the AI into treatment.

The ARISE method began evolving from the above mentioned approaches during the late 1970's and was formalized in the mid-1980's. Its development was primarily driven by families who refused to use the Johnson Intervention and the authors' interest in integrating systems theory with addictions treatment. The authors, concurrently with other researchers, found that the majority of families interested in getting a loved one into addictions treatment would not use the Johnson Intervention method for fear that long-term negative consequences would develop in the family's relationship with the AI.

Rather than viewing the families as being "wrong or uncaring" for not following through on the Intervention method offered, the authors decided to build on their knowledge of family systems, trust in family competence, strength and resilience, and family members' commitment to and interest in helping to get AIs into treatment. They developed and studied a new, simpler, and more cost-effective method.

An analogy for the development and progression of Invitational Intervention is the way in which engineers changed the design and ergonomics of seat belts. Initially, no one was prepared to wear a seat belt because it was viewed as a discomfort and a nuisance, with no evident or proven benefit. However, over the past 20 years, using a seat belt has become easier and easier to the point now of being second nature when one gets into a car. The empirically driven message that "seat belts save lives" inspired auto manufacturers to design a seat belt that would be used. Similarly, the authors know that Interventions save lives and were inspired to develop an Intervention method that would be more inviting, less intimidating, and therefore more likely to be used by more people.

Just as the use of seatbelts increased as their ease of use did, the authors found a similar response to ARISE. Most families, who were initially not interested in participating in an Intervention because of their preconceived notions, became interested and willing to use the Invitational Intervention method because of the openness and lack of confrontation that turned them away from the old methods. Families are aware of the attention given by ARISE to long-term family wellbeing and know that their ongoing relationship with their addicted member will be honored and protected. In other words, rather than blaming or labeling families for not intervening, the authors listened to what the families were saying, and incorporated their feedback into the development of Invitational Intervention——the ARISE method.

Integration of Systemic Thinking and Addiction

The key to understanding Invitational Intervention is to recognize the mechanism by which addiction and other symptomatic behaviors develop from unresolved grief and major or unpredictable loss. Realizing that the symptomatic behavior originated from Family Motivation to Change®, and that it began as a sub-conscious desire to protect the family from further pain and loss, allows clinicians and families to work collaboratively with hope and confidence toward long-term recovery. This systemic perspective provided by Transitional Family Theory provides a framework of healthy expectation and removes feelings of shame, blame and guilt, and simultaneously highlights and halts the inevitability of intergenerational transmission of the addictive patterns (see Chapters 3-4).

Philosophy

The success of Invitational Intervention and the ARISE method is based on an understanding of Family Motivation to Change and on a commitment to respect individuals and their families, their competence and inherent resilience, and their capacity to change and to heal. The collaborative partnership between a trained ARISE Interventionist and the Intervention Network is governed by integrity and a deep belief in the possibility of long-term recovery.

The following points summarize the basic tenets of the ARISE method:

- Individuals, families and communities are in constant transition. The more transitions experienced at any given time and the less resources available to deal with these transitions, or the less able the family is able to perceive or access the resources even if they are available, the more likely a problem will develop.
- Individuals, families and communities are intrinsically competent.
- Professionals, on their own, lack the resources and time to provide prevention and intervention services with families and communities needing help.
- Families are more powerful in effecting change than are treating professionals.
- Family Links (persons who play key connecting roles between professionals and the family network) have a real and meaningful stake in resolving identified problems. With minimal coaching, they are capable of accessing families who professionals may find very hard, or even impossible to reach, and of mobilizing the extended family and social support networks for problem solving more effectively than an outsider.
- By expanding the family network to help members be in touch with each other, always reconnecting as early as possible, but sometimes needing to make contact across lengthy "cutoffs" between family members, allows the family to access its competence while minimizing guilt, shame and blame.

- The Invitational Intervention process encourages family members to remain connected over time, and available to each other to resolve problems as they arise over time.
- The concept of "Less is more," or applying the minimum amount of effort, expense, and professional time, helps families realize they are capable of doing much of the work on their own.
- Given the proper balance of agency, guidance, support and opportunity, individuals, families, and communities will discover and use their unique strengths and competencies.
- Long-term recovery for AIs and their families is enhanced when issues of culture, gender and spirituality are taken into account, respected and addressed.

Practical Implications of ARISE Philosophy
Cooperatively Engaging with People Across Systems to Build Social Networks and Partnerships.

A powerful motivator for engaging the AI in treatment occurs when s/he realizes that bridges and collaborative relationships are being, or have been created among the people with whom she or he is involved on a day-to-day basis. When the Network is fully mobilized and united in its agenda, the AI is highly likely to enter treatment.

Owning a Sense of Competence that Relieves Guilt and Blame.

Understanding that the current addiction problem resulted from the intergenerational transmission of the original adaptive solutions from the past, allows that same drive of Family Motivation to Change to serve a positive problem-solving role in the here-and-now. Once blame and guilt are removed, the Intervention Network can be united toward a single sustained goal——getting the AI to engage in treatment.

Acknowledging, Building, and Shifting Accountability.

The closeness that develops from the building of the Network helps people realize that family members remain family members, regardless of whether they're talking to each other or not. They remain each other's primary relationships across time, and have responsibility and accountability for each other that are greater than that of other members of their social network, particularly the helping professionals.

Recognizing the Tension and Timing of Protectiveness Versus Autonomy.

For clinicians, learning how to choose when and how much to help the Intervention Network with the AI is a major challenge. The ARISE method provides for balance in this negotiation around problems and difficulties because of the built-in long-term accountability of the Intervention Network. No longer can the AI "call the shots" and manipulate individuals in the family or social network. S/he is part of the Network with a goal of solving a common problem. The Intervention Network is in charge and sets the rules for negotiation and monitoring of such issues as level of care, when to start treatment, involvement in self-help, and readiness to stop using.

The ARISE method may require that clinicians consider making a number of practical and philosophical shifts in their work with AIs and their families. The Step-by-Step guide provided in the following chapters is designed to support clinicians through these choices, and their subsequent Invitational Interventions.

PART II
Step-by-Step Guide to Invitational Intervention:

The ARISE Method

In this section of the book (Chapters 6-11) the authors present a practical guide to the ARISE method. The idea of presenting this Step-by-Step approach is to assist trained ARISE Interventionists in conducting an Invitational Intervention, and to offer other clinicians a detailed examination of the method with the idea that they would benefit from more formal ARISE training before actually proceeding to use it with clients.

The authors have provided case examples and detailed responses to situations that commonly occur when one is doing an Invitational Intervention. However, every family is different and each Intervention presents its own unique challenges and risks. The authors strongly suggest that Interventionists using an Invitational Intervention complete the two day ARISE training and have ongoing supervision, especially during the first four to six cases. Familiarity with the ARISE method and practice with the Invitational Intervention techniques build with time and practice.

The authors also have included two specific assessment instruments in Appendix A. The one for the addicted individual (AI) to use for self assessment is entitled UNCOPE: Questions to Screen Yourself for an Alcohol or Drug Abuse Problem. The second instrument entitled, UNCOPE: Questions to Family and Concerned Others to Screen for an Alcohol or Drug Abuse Problem, is useful for Concerned Others (CO) in their assessment of the seriousness of the problem and to help in their decision to move forward with an Intervention. The authors have also found it helpful to have ARISE Intervention Network members utilize the questionnaire for Family and Concerned Others to help underscore the seriousness of the problem, both for themselves and for the AI if s/he is present, and as a way of getting all members of the Intervention Network together on the same page. Used in this way, the instruments are valuable psycho-educational tools for the Interventionist and diagnostic indicators for the Intervention Network.

CHAPTER 6
The First Call

Overview of First Call

This Chapter will focus on Level I of ARISE, which starts when the First Caller, serving as a Family Link/Concerned Other, calls a facility or clinician (herein referred to as an ARISE Interventionist), to ask for help in getting an Addicted Individual (AI) into treatment. The First Call typically takes 20-30 minutes and is guided by a "First Call Worksheet" that provides protocols for the Interventionist to follow (See later in this chapter and Appendix A). The goals of the First Call are to: (1) ascertain that, given the circumstances, the CO has taken the correct action by reaching out with the call; (2) explain Invitational Intervention and the ARISE method; (3) identify potential members of the support group (herein referred to as the ARISE Intervention Network); (4) coach the CO as to how s/he can get a commitment from this Intervention Network to move forward; (5) develop the Recovery Message that will be part of inviting the AI to attend the first meeting, and (6) finalize the logistics for the first meeting.

Expanding the Referral Pool

Referral procedures between substance abuse treatment agencies and other systems, such as criminal justice and employee assistance programs (EAPs), are usually well developed. It will, however, take a new perspective on the part of the Interventionist, and new policies on the part of most agencies, to expand their referral pools, and to view COs such as spouses, parents, siblings, partners, friends, athletic coaches, co-workers or clergy as legitimate referral sources. Many treatment centers that require the AI him/herself to make the initial call to start treatment currently refuse to receive calls from COs. Fortunately, this practice is changing. Clinicians in the substance abuse treatment field commonly use various forms of leverage to get AIs into treatment, but are often hesitant to use the family itself as a source of persuasion. If this practice is not changed, many AIs and their families will be unnecessarily lost to the treatment system and will, as a result, have little hope of long-term recovery.

How the First Call is Similar to Employee Assistance Program (EAP) Referrals

Employee Assistance Programs (EAPs) provide an interesting parallel to the family/AI interface. The rationale for implementing EAPs was to intervene at an early point in a person's problem and to use continued employment as a motivating factor for change. The effectiveness of EAPs as leverage for treatment engagement has been established for a high proportion of working AIs. The analogy to the family/social network is that the CO functions in a manner similar to that of the supervisor in a job setting. Like the supervisor, the CO brings attention to the problem and initiates change. A treatment agency functions somewhat like an EAP—both the agency and the EAP are charged with taking rehabilitative action. The Figure below outlines the similarity of roles and functional interactions among the AI, supervisor, CO, EAP, and treatment providers. The ARISE method uses the leverage generated by the CO in the same way that the treatment agency uses the EAP generated leverage.

1. Problem is documented at work by supervisor	1. Problem behavior is recognized by the CO
2. Employee meets with supervisor and agrees to a plan for correction	2. CO expresses concern to AI
3. Warnings at work continue based upon monitoring of plan by supervisor; EAP is mentioned as part of an informal referral	3. CO admits to him/herself that the problem is more serious than AI is able to accept; treatment is suggested
4. Job performance improvements promised by employee are not kept	4. Promises from AI are not kept
5. Deteriorated job performance results in supervisor formally involving EAP for a job jeopardy intervention	5. Addiction worsens and CO contacts an ARISE Interventionist or treatment agency regarding an Intervention
6. Employee accepts treatment due to a potential consequence of job loss	6. AI accepts treatment due to pressure and consequences from the Intervention Network
7. EAP and supervisor coordinate the monitoring of job performance and treatment compliance	7. Intervention Network supports the AI in recovery process through continued meetings
8. EAP monitors employee as part of relapse prevention	8. Intervention Network monitors the AI as part of relapse prevention

Viewed this way, every First Call, regardless of the referral source, may be seen as the initiation of the ARISE process.

Barriers to Taking First Calls and How to Overcome Them

Substance abuse treatment program staff and private clinicians vary in their Intervention training and methods of accepting First Calls. Barriers to clinicians taking such calls include (a) counter transference based on experience with addiction in their own families, (b) agency procedures which require that the AI make the first call to "show motivation," (c) lack of Intervention trained staff, (d) restrictive reimbursement policies, (e) limited charting protocols, (f) concern about confidentiality violations, (g) clinicians who are already over-burdened with full case loads, (h) financial difficulties, and (i) difficulty changing from a therapy mode to a pre-treatment engagement process.

Many of these barriers to taking a First Call can be addressed by the agency administrator's making changes to policy and procedures, or through training and supervision. The ARISE method is designed to improve a treatment agency's capacity to reach a population of resistant substance abusers (typically not reached by traditional referral mechanisms), through that individual's family and social network. From a business standpoint, Intervention as a service is a generally untapped source of positive community marketing and new client referrals. However, because of the factors discussed above, pre-treatment is not often offered as a service by treatment agencies and an Intervention service will not work if it does not have the proper management and procedural support.

The Federal confidentiality rules (42 CFR, Part 2) do not apply to taking a First Call because there has been no actual contact with the AI, no chart has been opened, the information flow is coming from the CO, and the clients are the CO and Intervention Network. Thus, confidentiality is not an issue for these initial calls.

A Message to Agency Administrators:

The ARISE method is designed to improve a treatment agency's capacity to reach a population of resistant substance abusers through that individual's family and social network. This population of substance abusers is typically not reached by traditional referral mechanisms.

The National Institute on Drug Abuse (NIDA) study demonstrated that outreach efforts aimed at reaching family members and friends of addicted individuals resulted in significantly increased referrals. Outreach efforts can be employed creatively to involve the community in the referral process. Past efforts that have worked successfully include: involvement of clergy, notices in church bulletins, posters in hair salons, flyers distributed within paychecks, brochures in physicians' offices, business cards acknowledging the new program, and community presentations to high school parent-teacher groups. Outreach efforts need to be tailored to the specific locale and target population.

The authors' research has demonstrated, and their experience has further reinforced, that the process of implementing ARISE takes between two to four months depending on existing policies, size of agency, flexibility of staff, orientation of agency regarding working with families, and focus of current training/staff development programs. Practical matters which need to be addressed when implementing ARISE include: logistics to take First Calls, staff assignment and time allotment for ARISE related work, integrating systemic philosophy into the agency, arranging ARISE-specific supervision, designing and implementing a marketing strategy, and deciding what to charge for ARISE services.

Many agencies do not have fee schedules in place for pre-treatment (Intervention) services. Most insurance companies will not pay for Interventions, leaving the cost of an Intervention for the family and/or Intervention Network to bear. The authors have found that the cost for the Intervention is best discussed during the First Call. There is a wide array of cost options for an Intervention. For instance, some agencies use Interventions as a "lost leader" for marketing purposes. This means that the agency charges very little or nothing at all for an Intervention, because offering the service results in more referrals and the additional revenue generated from treatment offsets the cost of an Intervention. Other agencies charge on an hourly basis, and still others charge a one-time, all-inclusive fee. During the First Call it is common to suggest that the Intervention Network split up the cost of the Intervention, particularly if the Concerned Other is unable to carry the cost alone. No matter what is charged for an Intervention, the important point is to have the fee policy in writing so that Interventionists are guided in their responses to financial questions and that a clear contract exists between the Intervention Network and the Agency. (See Appendix for a sample Intervention Agreement that can be adapted to match specific Agency policies.)

In summary, administrative review of structure, policy and procedures related to a pre-treatment method are key to the effectiveness for implementing ARISE. Commitment to ARISE needs to come from the top down in the administrative structure. The authors' experience in the NIDA pilot study demonstrated that the ARISE model can be a morale booster in an agency because of the gratitude that concerned families express when the addicted individual engages in treatment. Staff members become enthusiastic about reaching a population that has been previously unreachable.

Bringing ARISE trained staff up to criterion in the model is important. The authors suggest that newly trained ARISE Interventionists and supervisors receive close supervision and monitoring by Certified Senior ARISE Interventionist Trainers for the first six cases. When three cases have successfully engaged in treatment, newly trained ARISE Interventionists become Certified ARISE Interventionists.

Taking The First Call: Completing The First Call Worksheet

This First Call can be taken by a psychiatrist or other mental health worker, primary care provider, social worker, substance abuse counselor, intake worker, member of the clergy, EAP counselor, or a receptionist who has received some basic training in ARISE. The same steps can be followed whether the CO is a family member, a friend, a co-worker, a landlord, or other concerned party. The First Call should ideally take 20-30 minutes, although those new to the method will probably take considerably more time until they are practiced and comfortable with the process. The First Call Worksheet guides the conversation. It is recommended that a copy of the First Call Worksheet be filled in as the Interventionist is taking the First Call.

ARISE FIRST CALL WORKSHEET

Caller's name:_____ Date:_____

Caller's phone #:_____ email:_____

Address:_____ Relationship to AI: _____

1. **Presenting Problem** (Join, Address Caller's Initial Concerns, Identify Presenting Problem)

2. **Get Permission to Ask More Personal Questions**

3. **Construct a Preliminary Genogram** (use back of this page or separate page)

4. **Construct list of support network members to invite to 1st meeting**

5. **Get Substance Abuse History**

6. **Get Brief Treatment History** (include self help, use of sponsor and any form of treatment received)

7. **Identify Past Family Efforts** (join around AI manipulation and breaking one-on-one isolation)

8. **Assess for Safety**
   a. Is the AI threatening to hurt him/herself or anyone else? (Are there weapons involved?)
   b. Has someone needed to call the police recently? (Explore details)
   c. Has the AI been involved in any serious accidents lately? (Explore details)
   d. Has there been any history of domestic violence or abuse?

9. **Finalize who to invite to form the Intervention Network and get commitment to attend regardless of whether or not the addicted individual attends**

10. **Finalize time and place to hold the First Meeting**

11. **Develop Recovery Message and strategy to invite the Addicted Individual**

Introduction of Interventionist

It is important to first introduce yourself by name and then use the title of "Trained Interventionist," subsequently stating that you specialize in working with families to get a resistant loved one into treatment. This introduction lets the CO know you are offering a service and will work with him/her toward the goal of getting the AI into treatment. Describe the Invitational Intervention continuum and the 3 Levels. Let the CO know that this call will be the start of Level 1 of the ARISE process. Have a copy of the First Call Worksheet available to use as a guide and fill it in for each First Call.

1. Presenting Problem: Identify What Precipitated the First Call

The next few minutes of the phone call are designed to understand the CO's reason for calling at this time: Why now? Ask for information regarding the background and context of the First Call to ensure that the problem identified by the CO matches the services you and/or your agency provide. For instance, if you work in a substance abuse treatment setting, you may not be trained to use the ARISE Intervention for an eating disorder. This initial screening determines the nature of the primary problem. If there is a match between the presenting problem and the service you provide, assure the caller that s/he has taken the right step and that you work with just this type of situation. This assurance begins to build hope and reduce fears. If not, then refer the CO to an appropriate professional or agency.

2. Join

After the reassuring statement, explain that this phone call will be used to discuss the current problems and explore options to deal with them. State that you will respect confidentiality by using first names only and will get more complete information if the CO decides to move forward with the process. Find out how the caller heard about you and/ or your agency, how familiar s/he is with the concept of Intervention, and whether s/he has 20-30 minutes to complete the initial information-gathering interview.

3. Validate the Addiction Problem and Get Permission to Ask More Questions

Summarize the presenting problem and validate the presence of a significant substance abuse problem. Reinforce for the caller the importance of this call and how instrumental s/he is in starting the process to help the AI get into treatment. Ask the caller for permission to obtain more personal information about the AI's family, friends and other supports, history of substance use, previous treatment and what the family has done in the past to deal with the problem.

This request for permission lets the CO know about the depth and scope of information you will be gathering so that it does not come as a surprise. It also is a good checking point to know if the CO has any hesitancy or ambivalence about moving forward. At times, stopping here to address any ambivalence allows the rest of the process to move smoothly, especially at points where a commitment is needed. This step prepares the caller for the nature of the questions to follow, communicates respect, and provides him/her with control over what is shared in the phone call.

4. Develop a Genogram Of At Least Three Generations

In order to gain a picture of the AI's family and broader social network, an initial genogram is helpful. While completing the genogram, the Interventionist develops an understanding of who is in the AI's nuclear and extended family, as well as the broader social support network.

Since the CO may be an employer or friend and not a family member, it might not be possible to develop a complete genogram. If this is the case, the CO is encouraged to identify as many members of the social network as possible, and to have a family member call the Interventionist so that the genogram can be completed. The more practice an Interventionist gets with using a genogram, the more useful it becomes to identify family scripts, themes and patterns that may be used in the development of the Recovery Message.

5. Construct a List of Support Members to Invite to the First Meeting

While developing the genogram, make a list of those individuals you would suggest be invited to attend the first and subsequent meetings. Remember to err on the side of inclusiveness because of the strong correlation between the number of individuals who are in the Intervention Network and the likelihood the AI will enter treatment.

The Interventionist can then draw on the information from the genogram to help advise the CO whom to invite to the First Meeting. Working together to create the genogram provides an opportunity to stress the importance of inviting as many people as possible to the initial meeting. The more people present for this initial session, the more likely it is the AI will come to the meeting and follow through by entering treatment.

6. Get a Substance Abuse and Brief Treatment History

Ask about the AI's current and past drug and alcohol use, focusing on information about acuteness and chronicity. This information will be used to help determine what level of treatment would be most appropriate and whether there are immediate medical concerns.

Obtain a history of the AIs substance abuse and psychiatric treatment (including current and past medications). Include any prior hospitalizations, periods of recovery, self help involvement, use of a sponsor, interest in, or development of new activities, perceptions of what made previous treatment successful and ideas of current relapse triggers or stressors that have not been addressed..

7. Identify Past Family Efforts

Find out what previous attempts have been made by the family to engage the AI in treatment. Acknowledge the love and concern the family has shown through these past efforts and listen for frustration and discouragement. Empathize with discouragement and inform the caller that it is easy to feel helpless and alone when dealing with an addict. Explain that the best way to help the AI is to assemble the people who care about him/her into an Intervention Network that works together first to get the AI into treatment and then to provide ongoing support for recovery.

8. Assess Safety

Obtain information regarding the AI's risk of harm to self, or to others. Ask the caller (a) if the AI is currently threatening, or has ever threatened, self-harm; (b) if the police have ever been called due to episodes of domestic violence; and (c) if the AI has recently been involved in any serious accidents. If the answer is "yes" to any of the above, explore in further detail to determine whether a situational crisis exists and assistance from emergency personnel is needed. If there is a risk of imminent danger, advise emergency action such as: bringing in additional family or friends to help, calling police, escorting the AI to an emergency department, removing weapons, etc.

9. Finalize Whom to Invite to Form the Intervention Network and Get Commitment to Attend Whether or Not the Addicted Individual (AI) Attends

At this point in the First Call, the Interventionist is bringing closure to the process. Get consensus on the final list of members to invite to the first meeting. If the CO is reluctant to invite key people identified, it may be necessary to go back to the points in Chapter 3 that deal with inclusivity. It is important to make sure that everyone invited, including the CO, makes a commitment to attend the first meeting whether or not the AI attends. The Interventionist can also extend an offer, conveyed by the CO, to any of the people invited to the first meeting to call or email the ARISE Interventionist if there are questions: If not, other issues, questions and concerns will be discussed at the First Meeting.

Experience has shown that starting the invitations with the "easiest" individuals (those less likely to be ambivalent about committing to come to the first meeting) and building from there is most successful. Often, more reluctant individuals are helped to get past the ambivalence when they hear who has already committed to attending the meeting. Keep in mind the single focus of the First Meeting: to get information out in the open about the AI's drug and alcohol use so that the seriousness of it can be conveyed to the Intervention Network and to the AI in order for the group to request that the AI start treatment.

10. Coach the CO to Prepare for a Variety of Responses from Potential Intervention Network Members.

The ARISE Interventionist can protect the CO from the anger, apathy, despair or rejection that might come as the result of inviting people to attend the first meeting. This can be done by predicting some of the negative responses that s/he may receive from the Intervention Network and the AI and rehearsing how to answer them. The Interventionist also needs to be prepared to be the target of blame, projected anger and fear. Often, fear is covered over with anger and threatening outbursts, which reflects polarized, black and white thinking. For example, if the AI comes to the first meeting and storms out halfway through, the Interventionist needs to be ready to be blamed for the "failure" and for "just making things worse."

It is important that the Interventionist be prepared for this type of outburst and handles it with calmness and composure, reflecting to the Intervention Network group that the AI is "testing us to see if we will give up on the process." Normalizing the AI's testing, and the initial blaming response by some of the group members, keeps the process moving and provides a powerful example of how the AI gets his/her way by acting out and displaying threatening behavior.

This normalizing response by the Interventionist also reflects to the group how important it is to stop the addiction from "running the show" and turn the fear into motivation to keep going. The successful handling of such outbursts also can be used in the future (see Chapter 8-Level 2) when more testing occurs by stating, "Here is more testing. Remember how well you handled it in that first meeting. Let's not give in now to the addictive manipulating. It has become clear that it is just a cover for how scared s/he is to take the next step in recovery."

11. Finalize Time and Place to Hold the First Meeting

There is great variation and flexibility about where to hold the first meeting. Some of the variation depends on the comfort of the Interventionist to do sessions outside of the office setting. There are always pros and cons to any choice of venue. The authors suggest that new Interventionists hold the sessions in an office setting until they have developed a comfort level with leading Invitational Intervention sessions. More seasoned Interventionists will be comfortable doing the first session wherever the CO thinks the AI would be most comfortable.

The authors commonly conduct Intervention meetings during business offices or after hours at the CO's home, at other relative's homes, at the AI's home, and in hospital rooms if the AI is hospitalized. The only significant caveat to the flexibility described above is if the AI has a history of violence. In that case, the authors suggest holding the Intervention meeting in an office setting during regular business hours, so that backup is available if needed.

12. *Develop Recovery Message and Strategy to Invite the Addicted Individual (AI)*

One of the most frequent questions that a CO asks an Invitational Interventionist is, "How do I invite my son, father, sister (the AI) to the session? What do I tell him/her this is about?" It is important to coach the CO to expect significant resistance around attending the meeting and to expect an argument about even having such a meeting in the first place.

First, it is important that the CO get a commitment for everyone invited to be part of the Intervention Network to attend the first meeting whether or not the AI attends. Once these commitments are in place, it is time for the CO (and others if it is appropriate) to invite the AI to the meeting. The authors suggest coaching the CO to follow the bulleted sequence below, keeping it short and to the point, without getting into a debate. After all, the meeting is taking place regardless of whether or not the AI attends:

- Decide whether it is best to issue the invitation alone or with others from the Intervention Network
- Choose a time to invite the AI when s/he will likely not be high or intoxicated. Preferably the invitation should occur a few days before the actual time of the meeting but not too far in advance or too close to the actual time of the meeting
- Start by telling the AI that there has been an increasing amount of concern and worry about his/her alcohol and/ or drug use and it has reached a point of concern where professional help has been sought
- Tell him/her that this concern and worry is shared by many people and the group is getting together (name the time and place) at the request of the professional "because s/he wants to hear everyone's point of view, including yours, about what is going on and to discuss options about what to do next"
- Provide the AI with the name, email, and phone number of the Interventionist who will be leading the meeting and let the AI know s/he can call or email with any questions

- Let the AI know that the meeting will take place whether or not s/he attends
- Identify all the individuals who have agreed to attend this first meeting
- Let the AI know that the goal of this process is to support him/her getting the help needed to stop the problem from getting worse
- If any negotiation takes place during the invitation, or there is clearly ambivalence about attending, suggest that the AI only come to the first meeting
- If the AI wants to argue or becomes defensive, do not engage with him/her on this issue, rather say that these would be good points to bring up at the meeting so they can be discussed with everyone present (Coach the CO to keep in mind that One-on-One, the AI always wins. This is the reason that the group is meeting.)
- Ask if the AI would like to ride with anyone who will be going to the meeting or if s/he would prefer to come alone
- Deliver the Recovery Message when it best fits into the invitation to attend the first meeting

A Recovery Message is a statement that is likely to hit at the heart of the problem for the AI and provide motivation to attend the first and hopefully subsequent meetings. As each Invitational Intervention case is different, so the Recovery Messages are different. The Interventionist may need to research two or three possibilities and ask the CO if one of them "hits home" and carries the emotional sincerity that s/he wants to convey.

The Recovery Message is developed from listening to the CO's information from the Genogram, past efforts the family has tried with the AI and any personal stories that describe the AI prior to the onset of addiction. The Recovery Message is so personal that it can only come from someone who has a detailed, usually lengthy history with the AI and is personally committed to encouraging and supporting change.

Following are some individual examples of Recovery Messages from cases with whom the authors have worked:

"You swore you would not drink like Dad because of the pain his drinking caused all of us. Now you are doing the same thing to your children. Let's not allow this problem to do the same thing to your kids that it did to us growing up."

"Let us help you get your life back and get your children back in your life."

"Ever since your husband died you haven't been yourself. You seem to be drinking a lot more and ultimately you can't drown your sorrows."

"We seem to have lost our brother (or son or grandson). We want him back. Remember those good times we used to enjoy? We miss you terribly. Let's get the good times back again without the drinking and drugs."

"You've changed so much over the past year or two. I don't even know you anymore. We used to be able to talk and now you can't even look me in the eye. We know you are not happy. Let us help you."

"We are really worried about you. You've been in hospital twice in the last few months and we all know that you're not well and that it's related to your heavy drinking even though you're trying to hide it from us. We're scared that you're going to die like Dad did from cirrhosis. Please work with us to get healthy again so you can be there for your children and not leave them like he left us."

Other Potential Outcomes from the First Call

Not all First Calls end with a commitment from the CO to move forward with the Invitational Intervention. Listed below are other outcomes that the authors have encountered from First Calls with suggestions on how to handle them.

1. If the CO made the call only to get information, it is usually best for the Interventionist to do a follow-up call after sufficient time has passed for the caller to have explored the Invitational Interventionist's website to get more information. This ensures a better opportunity to

assess the situation and answer questions or address issues that may be preventing the CO from moving forward at this time. It also provides a push that the family made need if they are ambivalent and scared to take any concrete action. Even if the CO decides to do nothing at present time, encourage him/her to call back in the future if the situation with the AI worsens. The authors typically make a second follow up call a few weeks later and, if necessary, yet another about a month after that.

2. If the CO and Interventionist were not able to complete all sections of the First Call Worksheet, schedule a follow-up time with the CO to complete the record.

3. If the CO completed the First Call Worksheet, but was unwilling to commit to setting up a first meeting or to inviting potential members of the Intervention Network without first speaking to them, the Interventionist should find out how much additional time the CO needs to contact the proposed members of the Intervention Network, and then set up a subsequent time for a follow-up call.

4. Should the CO complete the First Call Worksheet and then decide not to move forward at the end of the protocol, determine why s/he is not interested in moving forward. If the issues are not able to be resolved, ask if s/he is willing to talk again in two weeks and encourage him/her to call again if the AI's destructive behavior worsens in the future. Let him/her know that it is common to put the process on hold, as this keeps the door open, reduces feelings of blame/shame and sets up the next call. Find out if s/he is willing to have you call if s/he does not follow through on making the phone call.

5. If the CO either cancelled or needed to reschedule the first meeting, the Interventionist needs to call and find out what occurred to result in canceling the meeting. Often, it is simply a scheduling or financial problem, but it could reflect something more serious and if so the issue needs to be discussed.

6. Should the CO request a meeting alone with the

Interventionist or with the Intervention Network before deciding whether or not to continue with the ARISE process, it is usually a positive sign. Often, the individuals want to meet with the Interventionist in person, presumably to get questions answered, but more often they may want to make face-to-face contact to build trust. Once trust is established, it carries over to the first meeting. If this option is mentioned at the beginning of the First Call, a meeting can be set up with the Network to complete the First Call Worksheet in person. If both the Interventionist and the CO have time immediately, it is a good idea to meet so that initiating the process is not delayed.

In general, when difficult situations arise with either the family or the AI, the Interventionist should remain calm, reinforce that the Intervention is invitational, that there are no secrets, that it is being done out of love and concern, that there are reasons behind the addiction (it is not hopeless and the individual is not just a "bad apple"), that the method has proven successful, and that you as the ARISE Interventionist are there to offer your experience and knowledge, but that the family is at all times the real expert and is ultimately in control of the process.

It is just as important for the Interventionist to be prepared for multiple eventualities once work starts with a CO as it is to have the CO prepared for likely responses. The Interventionist builds confidence by handling difficult situations and successfully resolving complications over time. Each family presents with a different history and dynamics, yet it is this unpredictability that is part of the challenge, and the reward, for Invitational Interventionists.

CHAPTER 7
Conducting the First Meeting

At this point in the Invitational Intervention process, the Interventionist has completed the First Call Worksheet and has coached the First Caller, a Concerned Other (CO) member of the support system, serving as Family Link between the ARISE Interventionist and the Intervention Network, as to whom to invite to join the Network and how to invite the proposed members. The CO has also been coached regarding how to invite the Addicted Individual (AI), and to set up the First Meeting time and place. The ARISE Interventionist has a great deal of information, and more than likely, has not yet met any of the individuals who will be attending. It takes a leap of faith for the Interventionist to trust the next step.

This leap of faith is built on a number of the points previously covered; these points now need to be operationalized. They include: trusting that families are resilient, competent and intrinsically healthy; acknowledging the power in the force of Family Motivation to Change; viewing families as more influential in effecting change than professionals; and believing that the CO, now serving as Family Link, will be an effective bridge between the Interventionist and the family, and successful at connecting individuals across the Network and mobilizing them for problem solving.

The First Meeting typically lasts from 1½ to 2 hours. Goals of the First Meeting include:

- List and access family strengths;
- Get the topic of the AI's problems on the table so everyone is on the same page;
- Allow each person to talk about his/her concerns and if the AI is present, allow him/her to respond to the expressed concerns of the Intervention Network;
- Encourage the AI to enter treatment, and

- If the AI is not present, or is present and refuses to enter treatment, decide whether or not to go on to Level II.

A Step-by-Step Guide to Leading the First Meeting
The following points are meant to guide the Interventionist through this initial face-to-face meeting.

- Acknowledge the CO and then ask him/her to introduce you to the rest of the Intervention Network. Join with as many people as possible before the meeting starts. Observe family dynamics: are certain members excluded? Are others forming alliances? Are there any natural leaders in addition to the Family Link?
- If present, thank the AI for coming to the meeting, and acknowledge the courage it took to do so. Emphasize the importance of hearing each person's point of view about the problems, including that of the AI.
- Review pertinent details of the First Call and take responsibility for setting up the First Meeting. Explain that everyone present has come together out of love and concern for the AI.
- Set the agenda and the [generic] procedure for the meeting:
- Speaking directly to the AI, ask him/her if s/he would be willing to listen to what everyone has to say before responding;
- Solicit from each individual (if it is not volunteered) what his/her concerns are, and what s/he would like the AI to do
- Allow the AI an opportunity to respond, not only to the specifics related to the drug/alcohol use, but also to the requests to enter treatment;
- Work to get a commitment from the AI to enter treatment;
- If the AI agrees to enter treatment, coordinate the practical steps related to starting treatment;

- Get a commitment from the Intervention Network to meet again and to support and monitor the AI's commitment to the group, and
- Implement a plan for Intervention Network members to support each other, including the AI, during the time between meetings.

Case Studies: Scenarios and Strategies to Manage Them

The above procedure is generic because the steps apply across the board. The following scenarios are designed to provide the ARISE Interventionist with specific guidance for dealing with "real world" situations that might occur in First Meetings. However, nothing can replace experience and supervision to build confidence as an Interventionist and to develop a repertoire of responses.

The following case examples illustrate specific techniques, which may be useful in more situations than just the scenario presented.

Scenario I: The Addicted Individual Refuses to Attend the First Meeting

If the Intervention Network meets for a First Meeting and the AI does not attend, the Interventionist starts the meeting in the generic way as described above. However, rather than beginning by discussing the concerns of the group, first ask each person what contact s/he has had with the AI since being invited to attend. Include a more detailed description of the exchange between the CO and the AI at the time that the invitation was extended.

It is important for the Interventionist to ask the CO to present to the group the content of the Recovery Message and how the AI responded to it. This helps the Intervention Network determine whether it might be possible to contact him/her by phone from the meeting. The AI is often called on a high-quality speakerphone from the First Meeting and it is surprising how often s/he stays on the line for a large part of the session. If the AI does agree to the telephone conversation, then conduct the meeting by following the above steps as closely as possible.

If a phone call is not successful, then move to the phase of the meeting where each person shares his/her concerns, unveiling any secrets that may have been guarded by those closest to the AI. It is common to hear individuals comment, "I had no idea it was this bad." Getting everyone "on the same page" is essential because the Intervention Network will need to choose whether to stop meeting at this point or to continue on to Level II of ARISE to strategize how best to motivate the AI to enter treatment.

The more each member of the Intervention Network recognizes the importance of staying involved, the more likely the process will continue to move forward. This connectedness also supports each member of the Network by breaking the isolation and serves the critical purpose of presenting a united front to the AI. The principles demonstrated in this scenario are designed to break the secrecy, shame and guilt in the family as well as the isolation, and to give a message that the family can be creative in developing strategies to build motivation for treatment.

Scenario II: The Addicted Individual Plans to Attend "Only One" Meeting

In this situation the AI has made it clear that s/he will only come to one meeting. Generally, the ARISE Interventionist uses the generic procedure described above until the end of the meeting. After the AI has responded, most probably defensively, to the concerns expressed by members of the Intervention Network, the Interventionist takes the response and turns it back to the group for overall discussion. Typically, a lively discussion ensues because of the denial, minimization and rationalizations used by the AI. For most of the members of the Intervention Network this type of response has been heard before, and is perhaps expected. The radical difference is that now the discussion is open and no longer one-on-one. The Intervention Network feels empowered, rather than powerless.

There are times when the group will exert enough pressure and/or a sense of reality to result in is being possible to start meaningful negotiations with the AI. There are other times when the group concern is stonewalled. The Interventionist, after allowing appropriate time for discussion, stops the discussion (usually noting that the discussion has become redundant) addresses the AI, for example: "I have heard a number of serious concerns at this meeting about your drug and alcohol use. I know you say it is not a problem, but as recently as last month..."

Cite a specific example applicable to the AI, i.e., "You were arrested for a DWI and you were evicted for not paying rent. I know you don't think you have a substance abuse problem, but you must admit that something isn't right. If you are telling your family you won't go into a treatment program right now, what would you be willing to do?" If the AI begins to engage around the question "what *would* you be willing to do," take it as far as possible to get some commitment to change. The dynamic works this way:

- The AI states what commitment level s/he is ready to make, for example, s/he "will not allow it (party during the week and miss work) to happen again;"
- The Intervention Network states their skepticism but agrees to hold the AI to the commitment, with the proviso that the AI will go into treatment if s/he is not able to keep to the commitment;
- The Intervention Network agrees to a subsequent meeting (usually in two to three weeks if the situation is not critical, or earlier if it is) and invites the AI;
- The Intervention Network also makes a plan to monitor and support the AI for the interim two or three weeks.

The principle demonstrated in the case presented above is one of negotiating the beginning of a process. With ARISE it is possible to negotiate because the Intervention is a process occurring over time, with multiple meetings and a way to monitor the AI through ongoing built-in accountability to the Intervention Network. In this case, by the next meeting, the process had moved to Level II of ARISE.

Scenario III: The Addicted Individual Comes in Late to the First Meeting

This scenario occurs often. The authors believe the AI wants to hold on to some control in the process and some sense of autonomy and power. Being late makes the point that "whether or not I come to these sessions, late or on time, and whether I do anything about treatment is *my* decision."

The Interventionist should start the meeting as described in the scenario above where the AI refuses to attend. Regardless of what stage the meeting is at when the AI comes in, stop the process, make an introduction, and compliment him/her on the courage it took to attend. Let the AI know the individuals present were sharing their concerns and that you would like him/her to hear what everyone was saying before responding.

Proceed with the rest of the meeting using the steps outlined for conducting a session with the AI present. The principle for this scenario reflects respect for all participants inherent in the Invitational Intervention and is designed to proceed at the pace that the AI can tolerate.

Scenario IV: The Addicted Individual Leaves in the Middle of the First Meeting

This scenario is similar to the situation where the AI comes late to the First Meeting. Typically, the AI has heard a number of things during the meeting that increased his/her anxiety and fear. The addicted attitude and behaviors hover near the surface with most AIs and it does not take much for their fear and aggression to erupt. The acronyms for FEAR are ones that reflect both the addicted behavior (Forget Everything And Run), and what can develop in recovery (Face Everything And Recover).

What the AI does not yet realize is that storming out of the meeting actually has the exact opposite impact on the Intervention Network than s/he intended. Rather than frustrate and scare the group into stopping, storming out most often convinces the Intervention Network members how out of control the AI's behavior is, and how important it is for him/her to get into treatment.

It is crucial for the Interventionist to stay calm, check in with everyone to make sure that they are doing well, and provide support that addresses the possibility of their feeling any blame or guilt that could have the effect of breaking up the group effort. Staying united through the addict's acting out is a significant step in the family's healing as well as not letting the addiction dictate the outcome of events. It is also important for the Interventionist to be prepared for being blamed for the discomfort and disruption that occurred.

The Intervention Network needs to select which member will contact the AI, and design a Recovery Message that everyone will use when in communication with him/her. This situation provides an opportunity for the Interventionist to demonstrate how the acting out behavior was actually the addictive disease, not the AI him/herself. "S/he would never have behaved this way prior to the addiction taking hold." A typical Recovery Message would be "We know the pain you live with every day. What happened at the meeting wasn't the real you. We have seen you stop loving yourself over the past year and now we only see your anger and negativity. Let us help you get the joy back in your life that you used to have."

The principle demonstrated in this scenario is one of using whatever takes place in a meeting and working with it until a Recovery Message evolves. More of the psycho-educational teaching takes place in Level II sessions, but the First Meeting also provides some of the same teaching opportunities. Seeing the AI getting angry and leave the meeting early might discourage families who have lived with addiction for a long time. Be prepared to counter with stories of hope.

The Interventionist has the opportunity to change perspectives and empower the Network to access its own competencies. The Interventionist can stress the progress being made; after all, the AI did show up. Addictive and acting out behaviors are to be expected at this stage of the process. This scenario provides an opportunity for the family to remain in control over the addiction.

Scenario V: The Addicted Individual Comes to the First Meeting and Negotiates

This scenario is a very common outcome of the First Meeting and occurs when the AI is in the pre-contemplative or contemplative stage of individual change. Negotiating for "controlled" use allows the AI to move through the stages of change in a more directed manner because of the built-in accountability of the continued sessions as the Intervention Network monitors progress and makes suggestions regarding continued change.

If the Intervention Network and AI come to agreement on the specific meaning of "controlled" or "slowed down" drug and/ or alcohol use, then the ARISE Interventionist introduces the proviso that if the modified behavior is not sustained, then the AI agrees to go into treatment. For instance, the Interventionist may say, "I heard you agree to totally stop the cocaine use and I also heard you say that you wanted to keep drinking on weekends. Your family is appreciative of your openness to continue in this process, given how uncomfortable it is. However, your family is also skeptical that you will be able to drink on weekends and not eventually start using cocaine again. I would like to add a piece to the agreement—that is, your commitment to enter a treatment program if you start to use cocaine again."

At this point the AI can do little but agree because s/he is convinced the plan will work. The Intervention Network agrees to continue meeting, thus moving into Level II of ARISE. The principle demonstrated in this scenario revolves around the power of connectedness between family members and the AI. This connectedness allows for a negotiated outcome to the First Meeting and an open acknowledgement that many individuals in the Intervention Network are skeptical, but willing to stay involved in the monitoring process. The Interventionist takes on the spoiler role by introducing the proviso, if it had not previously been introduced. The Interventionist listens for what is not being said, breaks the silence, and has the opportunity to stretch polarities, introducing doubt and consequences, while at the same time modeling for the Intervention Network.

Scenario VI: The Addicted Individual Comes to the First Meeting and Agrees to Enter Treatment.

In this scenario the Interventionist uses the steps outlined above for how to conduct a First Meeting with the AI present. When the AI agrees to enter treatment it is important to discuss level of care with the entire group. As a starting point, the Interventionist must assess the need for inpatient detoxification. Second, if hospitalization is not needed, the question of using an inpatient rehabilitation program or outpatient treatment must be decided. The decision about level of care is not always up to the AI and Intervention Network due to the authority of managed care. This may need to be explained to the group.

Find out if the AI would like to go to the initial evaluation alone or with one or more members of the Intervention Network. When possible call the treatment facility and make the referral right on the spot. If a prior arrangement had been made with the inpatient program, discuss the logistics of getting the AI to the facility immediately after the meeting. If a time gap from when the meeting takes place to when treatment can start is unavoidable, develop a plan to help the AI manage that time. This may mean that s/he will stay with one of the Intervention Network members so a 24-hour safety watch can be maintained until treatment is started.

Discuss using self-help meetings as part of the treatment plan. Also set up the next Intervention Network meeting and make sure the AI understands that s/he is expected to continue to attend these sessions even after entering treatment, unless s/he enters inpatient rehab. The goal of future sessions shifts to supporting recovery, maintaining accountability for completing treatment and providing assistance to address early recovery issues. There should be weekly meetings for at least the first month the AI is in treatment.

This scenario exemplifies the power of families to guide change, and the importance of flexibility throughout the process of getting the AI started in treatment and providing support. The AI gets the message loud and clear that s/he is not alone in recovery. This is especially true with a chronic illness that is prone to relapse. The support in recovery can function as relapse prevention and can minimize the damage from relapse if one occurs because of the continued Intervention Network meetings that take place.

Scenario VII: The First Meeting is Completed and the Intervention Network Decides not to Meet Again

This scenario most commonly takes place when the AI does not come to the First Meeting or an unanticipated situation precludes having another meeting. The authors recently had two such situations occur. In the first case, the AI was arrested and was in jail at the time of the First Meeting. The Intervention Network came to a consensus in the meeting not to post bail, but rather to let the AI spend time in jail as a consequence of the drug use. The Intervention Network did not see any reason to hold further meetings until the AI was released. The Interventionist suggested meeting again closer to the time the AI would be getting out of jail so that treatment could be encouraged.

The second case involved an AI who got a job transfer around the time of the First Meeting. The Intervention Network met and agreed on a Recovery Message to deliver in writing to the AI, suggesting the need for treatment and the hope that it would be sought out in the new city. The Recovery Message also stated that the family had made a commitment to stop serving alcohol at family functions and the AI could expect alcohol-free holidays on future visits home.

Again, the Interventionist suggested the door stay open to getting together again in the future as the AI might reach out for help and the Network could easily be pulled together should that happen. The principle in this scenario is one of maintaining the hope that as long as the Intervention Network stays focused on its original goal, the strength of their commitment to the AI will eventually lead to long-term recovery. The message conveyed also underlines the flexibility of ARISE, and the working principle that an Invitational Intervention is a process, not a one time event.

Closing the First Meeting

The Interventionist closes the First Meeting with a summary reviewing what agreements have been made and including what steps will be taken next. Everyone is encouraged to support one another so that no one person has to make any decision in isolation. If pressured by the AI, Intervention Network members should make use of the Recovery Message and let the AI know that all future decisions will be made by group consensus.

Prepare the Intervention Network for the possibility that the AI might contact one of the Network members in a desperate time of need. Assure them that this type of reaching out is not unusual, and that it should be immediately relayed to the rest of the Network. Encourage ongoing contact with the AI and repeated stating of the Recovery Message. Make sure everyone has your business card and feels free to contact you without hesitation. Let the group know that at future Level II Meetings, a review will take place looking at what worked and what did not work, thus guiding future strategies to successfully motivate the AI to enter treatment.

Finalize the next date and time for the Level II Meeting and end on an encouraging note that has hope and builds on the family's strengths. The more Level 1 cases successfully completed, the less it will feel like the Interventionist is taking a leap of faith. Instead, faith in the competence, resilience and intrinsic health of families becomes second nature.

DR. JUDITH LANDAU AND JAMES GARRETT

CHAPTER 8
Level II: Strength in Numbers: The Intervention Network

As discussed in previous chapters, the ARISE method empowers families by helping them recognize and harness their resilience, inherent strengths, resources, and commitment to help their recovering person succeed in the world after treatment. In Level II——Strength in Numbers——the positive and respectful aspects of Invitational Intervention are most evident. The natural influence and commitment of family, friends, co-workers, and other social support network members are mobilized to motivate a resistant addicted individual to enter treatment.

The primary emphasis of Level II is to maintain the focus of the Intervention Network—treatment engagement, ensuring that the addicted individual (AI) knows that there will be no further opportunities for splitting, manipulation, isolation or disempowerment. The Network makes a commitment to reach consensus and speak with one voice to ensure there will be no question about this primary goal. During Level II a wider perspective on the problem and its context is taken and members gain a more complete picture of what has transpired with the AI.

The AI has been invited to the Level I First Meeting and knows that the group has made a commitment to meet whether or not s/he attends. Level II can consist of one to five face-to-face meetings with the Intervention Network, including most of the individuals who were part of the Level I meeting, and may or may not include the AI.

If the AI comes to the first Level II meeting and is interested in entering treatment, the initial session is conducted as an evaluation (similar to the Level I First Meeting when the AI attends. (See Chapter 7)

Expanding the Network

Usually, Invitational Interventions gradually build momentum. When working with only one, two or three people, the Interventionist focuses on ways to expand the Network. The Interventionist can encourage the participants to use this first Level II meeting to call family or friends who are significant to the addicted individual, via a telephone conference using a speakerphone which allows key persons who otherwise would not have been present to take an active part in the Intervention Network meeting.

A return to Level I steps may be necessary to help the present Intervention Network members expand the list of potential participants, in preparation for building a larger, more representative Network. When the Interventionist recognizes the Network members' frustration at not engaging other members and helps plan who will be called next, this effort encourages them all to remain committed to the ARISE process. The Interventionist can role play with the Intervention Network Members how best to deal with troublesome reactions which may arise such as anger, apathy, despair, or rejection.

Regardless of how many people participate in the initial meetings, the Interventionist listens to the in-session conversation with an ear toward planning whom else to include, and how best to broaden the Intervention Network. Taking an all-inclusive point of view toward expanding the Network will show the AI that s/he can no longer get to people "one-on-one." In addition, expanding the Intervention Network ensures that no one person experiences burnout, and always has someone in the group to call on for support.

The preliminary genogram from the First Call is helpful in expanding the original contact list, as is the construction of a social communication flow chart, which identifies how members of the potential support network interact. This information can determine which Intervention Network members are to be contacted for the next meeting, and who most likely be successful at convincing them to attend.

The Level II Strength in Numbers First Meeting

Although this intervention process is for *engagement into* treatment only (and not treatment), it is still necessary to gather information as to insurance coverage and the history, nature and extent of the addiction in order to guide decisions about level of care and appropriate treatment referral.

1. *"Joining" Each Member of the Network*

The Interventionist adapts his/her "joining" style to fit the style of the particular family. If the Intervention Network members talk noisily among themselves in a disorganized manner, the Interventionist will need to provide direction for the meeting. If the Network is withdrawn and quiet, the Interventionist will respectfully need to draw out members, always thanking them for attending and encouraging them to share their concerns.

The authors have found it best to first greet the First Caller, who, as described in earlier chapters may serve as Family Link between the family and the professional or agency. The Family Link is the member of the family and/or support network who knows everyone best, has most contact with most members and is most acceptable to the majority, is the least polarized or caught in coalitions, and has, most probably, ensured that everybody came to the session. The First Caller is also identified as a Concerned Other (CO) member of the social support network, so is automatically framed in a positive light from all angles. The First Caller, or CO, then introduces the Interventionist to members of the Intervention Network whom s/he has not previously met. To create a comfortable and informal atmosphere, members who have not seen each other for awhile are encouraged to visit with each other for a few moments.

One of the first tasks is to help the Intervention Network understand the importance of being open with the AI in order to avoid secrecy and coalitions. The Interventionist should mention that it is normal to feel varying emotions while discussing difficult topics, which may never have been shared openly before. When the Interventionist follows the Invitational Intervention guidelines, anxieties will be reduced and participants will begin to feel more comfortable being genuine and spontaneous with each other. Remind them they are meeting because they care about the AI and the family.

When the AI is present, the Interventionist makes a special effort to engage him/her in conversation, and listens carefully for subtle hints in the conversation to ensure that s/he does not come under attack during the meeting. Some members of the Intervention Network present may

try to subvert the process in order to show how "bad" the AI is, or has
been. Be prepared to counter this with positive statements about the
courage it took for the AI to attend the ARISE meeting.

2. Eliciting Family Strengths

Families who live with substance abuse or other addictive behaviors
have often been "through the mill" by the time they meet with the
ARISE Interventionist. They may feel guilty, ashamed, and blamed—
both by themselves and others—for the problems in their families.
There is a circular causality in families with addicted members—the
family is affected by the addiction and the family affects the course of
the addictive disease. For change to happen, each family needs to believe
change is possible. Even though dysfunctional patterns exist, during the
family meeting the Interventionist stresses that, like all families, this
family is intrinsically healthy and competent. When family strengths
are identified, the Intervention Network begins to understand how the
development of the addiction was in an attempt to preserve the family,
rather than destroy it. Shame, blame, and guilt are reduced and the AI
becomes more motivated to enter treatment.

In Level II meetings, this exploration of family strengths may be
accomplished by creating a list on a flip chart that will later be used for
the engagement process. The list is drawn from the intergenerational
families of origin, extending back into their past, and including their
stories of migration, overcoming hardships, survival, and endurance.
When there are younger people in the room, it is often useful to invite
them to be scribes and their participation spurs the family on to share
more of the pride in their past. There is always a story of grief and loss
and love.

Explaining how all families are constantly in transition and vulnerable
during times of change, and go through both good times as well as times
of hardship and testing helps to eliminate the "we/they" dichotomy. In
the process of identifying family strengths, the Interventionist speaks
of the courage it took for the First Caller or CO to initiate the process,
as well as the courage of the family in coming together to address the
painful issue of addiction. The Interventionist draws the analogy with
the strengths of generations past and talks about the survival skills and

courage of this family. Hearing messages of praise and achievement, the family begins to accept its own competence.

During a crisis, when families have lost hope, it is difficult for them to see the strength and resilience they have shown in previous crises. The following case illustrates the process of eliciting family strengths as well as illustrating the principle of "Strength in Numbers."

The Case of Malcolm

Malcolm had dropped out of treatment after his twelfth hospital-based detoxification. A hotel manager called Malcolm's ex-wife to say that he'd been found unconscious in a bathtub and was rushed to the hospital where it was a touch-and-go situation for several days. Malcolm had overdosed on a combination of alcohol, sedatives and street drugs. Afraid Malcolm would die, his ex-wife called an ARISE Interventionist. She was coached on ways to invite as many members of his support network as possible to discuss strategies on how to get him from the hospital into treatment.

The first Level II meeting included Malcolm's ex-wife, his mother, father (a long-time active alcoholic), great-uncle, siblings, children, and his employer. Understandably, the Intervention Network felt overwhelmed, terrified, and immobilized by the imminent threat of Malcolm's death, or the very real possibility of long-term permanent paralysis and/or vegetative state from serious brain injury. They were only able to think in terms of crisis, deficits, and dysfunction. It would be difficult for the Interventionist to focus on the task of uncovering the existence of any family strengths.

During the session, with the help of the Interventionist, they began to realize that Malcolm's current crisis was not the only cause of their current fears and immobilization when a "horrible history" of multiple catastrophic deaths in the family was revealed. With the Interventionist's prompting, the family began to appreciate the impact and challenges of previous intergenerational losses, which had actually helped their ancestors develop survival skills. The family reconstructed the continuity of its own Transitional Pathway and were feeling encouraged by the many strengths and resources that were revealed as the family continually met its challenges over generations.

The Intervention Network began thinking about positive outcomes when members realized that there was hope for the future and that they were not to blame. They thought in terms of "strengths and resources" when they considered how they might proceed toward treatment engagement and, most importantly, what family strengths they would like to see handed down to future generations. Their list included family loyalty and protectiveness, a "hard-work" ethic, a pioneering spirit, a love of music, and many others.

With the Interventionist's guidance, the Intervention Network planned for Malcolm's return should he regain consciousness. After four meetings, the Network heard that Malcolm had turned the corner and was regaining consciousness and mobility. Some weeks later when Malcolm was discharged, the family was able to implement their strategies for his engagement into practice, and he re-entered treatment, this time with the long-term support of his family and their belief that he would succeed.

3. Constructing a Genogram

After listing family strengths, the ARISE Interventionist and the Intervention Network construct a genogram (see Appendix I), expanding on the knowledge disclosed during the First Call. The Interventionist explains the purpose of doing a genogram, then, with the assistance of the family, constructs it on the flip chart, asking senior family members to provide information about previous generations of their families. It is helpful to go as far back as possible, since the losses where the original addictive behaviors first manifested might be as removed as three-to-five generations.

The genogram accomplishes several things: (a) allows those present to think more broadly about potentially important players; (b) helps them think of ways to enlarge and mobilize the extended support system; (c) enables access to additional competence across the system; and (d) prevents members from getting caught in their own perspectives, old alliances, and triangles.

The genogram allows family members to explore losses and "cut-offs" that may have resulted in not having access to some members' competencies which might have been useful in difficult times. The genogram provides a visual chart of potential Intervention Network support that can be mobilized to help get the addicted individual into treatment. This "reconnection" is often highly effective in its own right. Addicted individuals are often part of the "cut-off" pattern. Reviewing the visual family genogram, the Interventionist and the Network can hypothesize and understand why it has been so difficult to get the addicted AI into treatment until now. New strategies to engage the previously resistant addicted individual can be planned.

4. Reviewing Previous Efforts to Engage the Addicted Individual in Treatment

The AI may or may not have been present for the Level I first session or involved in any previous efforts to engage him/her in treatment. The Intervention Network invariably learns that most prior attempts at engagement were one-on-one confrontations with the AI and that this Level II network meeting may be the first attempt at a partnership or teamwork. This underscores the realization that dealing with the AI on a one-on-one basis is bound to fail.

5. Eliciting Statements of Concern about the Addiction From Each Member

The Intervention Network is assured by the Interventionist that s/he plans to be supportive and available between meetings by telephone if necessary. The Interventionist also explains that meetings will be safe, positive and goal directed, and informs the network of his/her general experience in dealing with difficult situations. Mutual respect between the Interventionist and Intervention Network members is important, as is the support Network members will give each other when painful topics are discussed. Circular seating arrangements and other use of physical space can provide a feeling of welcome and security. The Interventionist stresses that sessions will be held whether or not the AI attends.

Everyone's concerns and reasons for attending will be presented. If the AI attends the meeting, it is always helpful to praise him/her for taking the risk to attend. Whether the AI talks before or after the others, the Interventionist is acknowledging his/her autonomy, and reassuring the family that s/he will be treated with respect. The AI's reactions to his family's concerns are always worth noting. The Interventionist needs to ensure that s/he either hears, or is made aware of, the family's assurances of love and caring. As a safety caution, the Interventionist must get a commitment from everyone that there will be no physical or verbal abuse during the meeting for the safety of every member present, saying "Can we all agree on that?"

This openness and balance of the preceding discussion counteracts any possibility that the AI will feel coerced into treatment. S/he is likely to feel relieved to finally be able to honestly discuss things with everyone. When the AI is not present, the session proceeds in a similar manner. Statements of concern evolve into motivational strategies for change and treatment engagement.

6. Discussing the Addicted Individual's Denial and How to Adapt Engagement Strategies

If the AI is present at the first Level II meeting, and denies a problem or attempts to block discussion of the problem, the Interventionist can use this as an opportunity to discuss how the denial process is similar to what network members experience in their everyday lives and proceed with their assistance through the denial. The Intervention Network is always ready to give examples of the "stinking thinking" of the addicted individual, and how s/he always, "shoots him/herself in the foot." For example, in one session, a mother complained that her daughter always drank too much and then overslept on the days of important job interviews. The daughter would then deny being hung over the next morning, and her excuse for missing the interview was, "They wouldn't have hired me anyway, so why should I have gone and been humiliated?"

If the AI is not present—a more common scenario—the session is conducted in a similar manner, with each person describing the problem. The Interventionist congratulates the network members on their efforts to engage him/her, and encourages them to describe what they tried and what role the First Call played. In the face of apparent early failure, the Interventionist normalizes the difficulties, taking responsibility and acknowledging that there might have been something more s/he could have suggested during the First Call. Even with this approach, the Intervention Network members may initially feel responsible for the AI's absence. Their sense of guilt will provide yet another barrier to the process of engagement.

Once the Intervention Network gains an understanding of how difficult it is for the addicted individual to acknowledge the need for help, the members feel freed up to start thinking of creative solutions of how to invite him/her to the next meeting. By predicting the difficulties usually encountered in dealing with the AI's denial and reinforcing that this process often takes several attempts, members of the Intervention Network feel less discouraged and overcome by their own self-doubt. This process also helps to counter their anger, frustration and blame of the addicted person. All their efforts will become the foundation for the important work of developing further strategies. Whether the AI engages in treatment or not, the support network is encouraged to meet on a biweekly or monthly basis as needed.

It might seem surprising that families would continue to meet as long as two or three months without the AI's entering treatment. However, it is the authors' experience that families tend to continue because of their investment in the outcome, and because of the positive changes they themselves are experiencing in their communication and relationships. Their discouragement and despondency is being steadily replaced by hope, and a sense of empowerment, where before there was helplessness.

7. Determining Patterns of Alliance

If the AI is present, the first task is to protect him/her from attack. This requires paying close attention to which network members ally with or against the AI's need to enter treatment. Apart from this, the meeting proceeds similarly, whether or not the AI is present.

The Interventionist starts this step by reiterating to the network members what they have accomplished to date. Perhaps the greatest challenge in Level II is remembering that this is not a therapy session, but a pre-treatment engagement Intervention with the sole objective of motivating the AI to enter treatment. This is a time when the

Interventionist does not share his/her findings with the Intervention
Network, but instead uses them for his/her own guidance. Information
gathered through observation needs to govern the Interventionist's
thinking, but not necessarily be shared with the Intervention Network
until the time is right.

During this part of the meeting, the Interventionist watches for
how members relate to each other, what collaborations and exclusions are
formed, how each member participates in the engagement attempts, and
looks to identify each person's point of view, their responses, and their
positions taken regarding engagements. S/he is looking to identify natural
leaders and potential allies of the CO/Family Link. The Interventionist
particularly notes: which Intervention Network members take strong
positions about issues; who, if anyone, takes a leadership role, and when
differences of opinion arise, who acts as mediator.

S/he looks for the Intervention Network's ongoing patterns of
alliance, their sub-groups and hidden coalitions. The identification of sub-
groups, alliances and coalitions provides insight and guidance about who
to include and prepares the Interventionist for which network members
might take particularly strong positions about issues and who is likely
to side with or against them. An observant Interventionist can sense the
beginning of conflict and is ready to support a potential mediator before
the conflict is apparent to the rest of the Intervention Network or the AI,
and before any real damage has occurred.

The Interventionist's responsibility is to keep the Intervention
Network focused on the goal of treatment entry for the AI. The case
below is an example of the Invitational Interventionist being aware of
possible allies of the CO/Family Link and working to increase their level
of involvement.

The Case of Harry
Harry and Carol had been married for twenty-five years, during
most of which Harry had been an active alcoholic. A long-time
member of AA, he had never been sober for longer than a couple
of months, despite many attempts at treatment. He was now on
the brink of losing his long-term job because his employer and
close friend could no longer protect him. Harry had advanced
liver disease, peripheral neuritis and early cognitive loss.

Carol was an extremely competent woman who "held things together" at the office she managed. Carol's competence and control, so evident at the office, failed her in the home. Her two adolescent children were constantly in trouble at school, and both her brother and sister had grown tired of discussing her problems, since she apparently never followed-up on their advice. She felt that she had nowhere to turn and finally called an ARISE Interventionist for advice.

She was subsequently asked to invite all the members of her support network to an ARISE Intervention session. Her brother and sister refused to attend, but the rest of the family members came. Carol's growing isolation and inability to feel supported had caused her to become easily irritable, instigating her children to align with their father. They blamed their mother for all the problems, saying they understood why their father drank, and that they couldn't wait to get out of the house.

A plan was made for the Invitational Interventionist to invite Carol's brother and sister to the next session, telling them that if Harry were fired, it would result in their sister being out on the street. They came to the session and, for the first time, as Carol started to weep, her brother and sister and Harry's employer began to realize the depth of her despair and hopelessness. What they had previously experienced as nagging and bossiness was clearly based on the fear that Carol had always managed to cover up with her pretense of apparent control.

The Intervention Network decided that Carol needed more support in setting limits and establishing constructive consequences should Harry continue drinking. At the fourth session, as a group with one voice, they informed him that he would lose his job, his wife, and his children if he refused to go into treatment. Harry went to the hospital that day.

The setting of limits, and Carol's receiving support from her siblings for the very first time, marked a major shift from Carol's previous sense of complete isolation toward her feeling supported and then being able to become effective. The new alliance enabled the Intervention Network to reach its goal of getting Harry into treatment while also strengthening family ties. These sessions were supportive, loving and goal-oriented. At no point were there secrets or surprises. Harry was invited to each session, and included and kept informed of the process throughout, even when he did not attend sessions. When limits and consequences were set, he was involved in the negotiations.

8. Developing Strategies for Motivating the Addicted Individual toward Treatment Engagement

If the AI is present, this initial session evolves into a motivational meeting aimed at getting a commitment from him/her to begin treatment and to meet with the Intervention Network (typically one week later) to report on progress. If this is not completed during the meeting, the Intervention Network continues to meet with the AI (typically, once or twice a month) until treatment is started.

If the AI elects not to attend the meeting, the ARISE Interventionist, based on the family's strengths and previous experience, assists the Intervention Network to identify a range of options that lead to natural strategies for engagement. This keeps the Interventionist focused on the single goal of engagement and avoids the session turning into treatment. The possible approaches are designed to match the level of resistance and denial shown by the AI. A component of these strategies always includes inviting the AI to the next session. The Intervention Network benefits from the engagement process regardless of its outcome (i.e., whether the AI enters treatment or not) since it results in improved communication, an airing of prior difficulties, a forging of new collaborative relationships, and a belief in their competence as change agents.

The Intervention Network is constantly reminded that they are at the meetings because they truly care about the AI. Each member is asked to propose ideas to the group and then asked to discuss and process them. The Interventionist guides the progression to obtain a consensus. The members of the Intervention Network are asked to identify practical tasks that can be implemented should problems arise such as if the addicted individual disappears; a member decides that the task is too great and resigns; the negotiation does not go well, or feelings of anger, frustration, or fear promise to sabotage the process.

The Invitational Interventionist guides the Intervention Network to identify concrete strategies, such as planning how they will make contact with the AI and identifying who specifically will call him or her or who will write a letter. In preparation for the next session, members are directed to investigate possible treatment programs and all the details about costs, bed availability, and any other questions that they would like to have answered.

One possible complication that the Network should be aware of when developing treatment engagement strategies is the possibility of a "partner in crime." The AI often has a friend, spouse, or significant other who also abuses substances and the AI may use this relationship as a counterbalance to the pressure of getting treatment. Discuss specific ways for providing support and companionship, and filling the gap left by the loss of any relationship in the event the AI needs to refrain from seeing their "partner in crime."

It is crucial that the Intervention Network find out if the AI's living situation is stable and supportive enough to help him/her stop the addictive behavior, the use of alcohol, chemicals, or both. If it is not safe, a 24-Hour Safety Watch needs to be implemented; those who are available to do so should be identified at this point. A Safety Watch always includes a number of people being with the AI in "shifts," so that the burden is not fully placed on one person.

9. Negotiating With the Substance Abuser and Intervention Network to Make a Formal Contract.

A key aspect of the ARISE process is helping the Intervention Network negotiate with the AI to make a formal agreement around the primary goal of getting him/her into treatment. This typically involves important decisions about the level of care that will be required and a timetable for when treatment will start. The Interventionist works with the Intervention Network to determine what the AI is willing to do for treatment and then to respond to his/her proposal.

Members of the Intervention Network frequently polarize around this topic, taking different positions about location, type of facility, level of care, and length of stay. It is important to assist the Network to reach consensus. One method to achieve this is by using the technique of Transitional Strategic Polarization: Each member of the Intervention Network states her/his position along the continuum between the poles. The continuum is drawn on a flip chart and either the Interventionist or members of the Intervention Network apply dots to represent their positions. Initially, there are often extreme differences in the positions. Contingencies can then be created for each potential position on the continuum.

For example, as demonstrated in the following case, perhaps the AI is bargaining for some vacation time before going into treatment, and some network members may be pushing him/her to go for outpatient treatment, while others may insist that s/he be admitted for inpatient treatment. The continuum would then progress from the least stringent, and clearly ridiculous proposal for treatment—a vacation on a cruise ship, to the next level consisting of outpatient treatment, and finally to the most stringent option suggested—admission to an inpatient treatment facility.

The Intervention Network is encouraged to debate their decision. As the discussion heats up, which it invariably does, the Interventionist participates in the debate, fanning the flames by accentuating the discrepancy between the poles, and helping each person who is upholding the opposite polar position make his/her opponent's thinking appear to be absurd. This is illustrated by the case of Miranda described below. The process of stretching the poles to the point of absurdity allows the Intervention Network members to soften their positions and to think more reasonably about the real options.

Inevitably they swing together towards a more reasonable consensus and assemble new positions close enough to the midline to reach consensus and make a firm decision about treatment choices. A formal network contract is then negotiated and signed, specifying the responsibilities of both the Addicted Individual and the Intervention Network (For examples, see Appendix A: Sample ARISE Intervention Network Agreement, and Sober Support Intervention Network Agreement).

The Case of Miranda

Miranda, at age sixteen, despite being grounded for her poor school grades, missing class on numerous occasions, and finally, being caught with cocaine in the school restroom, tried very hard to persuade her parents to let her go with her classmates for a spring break cruise. She begged and pleaded with her parents, almost convincing her mother that, "her life would be over," if she missed this, "one and only ever in a lifetime special event."

Miranda's mother called an ARISE Interventionist for advice and was coached to bring as many members of the support network as possible to the First Call meeting. She was convinced that Miranda would refuse to come, but the Interventionist assured her that in his experience adolescents are naturally both curious and controlling. He predicted that Miranda would not want to miss out on the action, and would want to know what people were saying about her once she knew that the meeting would be held, regardless of whether or not she attended. He also predicted that she would think she could convince them of her logic if she had the people who loved her, those she had always successfully manipulated, in the meeting.

Attending the meeting were Miranda's maternal grandmother, her mother and father, an uncle, and her younger brother. Miranda also brought along a classmate for support of her position. Miranda charmed and cajoled. With typical adolescent grandiosity, Miranda began to offer bargains, which proved irresistible to her parents, ranging from promises of endless sobriety and perfect grades to babysitting her brother, watering the plants, and even emptying the kitty litter boxes when she returned from the cruise, if she were to get her way. She promised to sign up for outpatient treatment the minute she returned.

Miranda's uncle, on the other hand, who was in recovery from serious alcohol abuse for the past seventeen years, insisted that she immediately be admitted to inpatient treatment to avoid her becoming seriously addicted. He wanted her to have an opportunity to "nip it in the bud before her life is wasted as so much of mine was." Her parents felt utterly defenseless and were about to capitulate to their daughter's tears, when the matriarch, the maternal grandmother, began to speak firmly.

The grandmother spoke of her own youth, and how promises were easy to make, and just as easy to break. She pointed out that none of Miranda's grand offers started prior to the spring break trip, and asked why that hadn't alerted her parents that

Miranda was most likely being less than honest. She also pointed out that Miranda had minimized, if not outright lied, about the extent of her alcohol and drug abuse.

In clear terms, the grandmother took over the coaching, setting firm consequences for Miranda. She assured her daughter and son-in-law that Miranda was being manipulative and had no intention of stopping her drug use. She reminded everyone that cruise ships were notorious for alcohol and drug use; Miranda was not planning to go on a geriatric voyage! She suggested that Miranda's promise to be "good" after the cruise was not an accurate predictor of how she intended to lead her adult life.

When the Intervention network reached consensus that action needed to be taken, the network members set clear boundaries for Miranda, informing her there was still time before the trip to prove herself by agreeing to an alcohol and drug evaluation, and starting an outpatient program immediately, if that recommendation were made. Miranda was told that if she reneged on the agreement, she would be grounded and miss the cruise. She also was told that if she failed to follow through on the agreement for an evaluation and outpatient treatment, she would be hospitalized in an inpatient program and miss the cruise altogether.

Miranda's parents were grateful to the grandmother for her role modeling. They expressed amazement when Miranda said she felt relieved to have clear boundaries set for her, and to know where she stood. Miranda chose to stay with her grandmother for part of the holidays. She explained that she loved her grandmother deeply and knew she could always rely on her to tell the truth, "Exactly the way it is." The negotiation in this example resulted in a contract, including a sequence of consequences as well as rewards, with Miranda having the choice to stay with her grandmother during the holidays and the opportunity to prove herself so that she could go on the cruise.

Contracts are best carefully written out, with everyone's signature to indicate agreement with all the terms. There will then be no contesting what everyone has agreed upon. The written contract should include specific details, such as where the treatment will take place, when it will begin, and how long the AI has agreed to commit to it. When there is a deadlock in preparing the contract and an important family member is not present, that person needs to be contacted. The input of another key person will often allow the family to move forward.

Conventional wisdom discourages negotiation with the AI. This belief stems from many failed negotiations with substance abusers, usually conducted one-on-one with the abuser who was desperately bargaining his/her way out of changing drinking and drugging behaviors. Because the ARISE process of negotiation includes an Intervention Network, there is always someone to do a reality check. The AI is held accountable for any promises made. The Intervention Network designs appropriate consequences for any lapses, and decides how, and who will enforce those consequences. AIs frequently enter treatment at this stage and the engagement process is complete.

10. Preparing Intervention Network for Handling Possible Crises

Prior to ending a Level II meeting, the Interventionist needs to ascertain that the Intervention Network is prepared to handle any possible crises that may arise. If the AI is present, the Interventionist might show compassion to him/her for having been put in this difficult position, and remind him/her that what is happening is a result of how much the network members care. The AI is most likely feeling threatened, angry, scared, or backed into a corner and should be encouraged to let the other Network members know how s/he is likely to "act out" or otherwise express these feelings.

If the AI denies any negative feelings saying there is no chance of acting out behaviors as a result of the meeting, the Interventionist should explain that it is usual for the AI to place some type of pressure on Network members. Examples might be refusing to attend the next meeting, deciding to quit on his/her own without treatment, to begin or continue using, and/or to threaten suicide or violence. The Interventionist then can ask the Intervention Network whom the AI is most likely to call or pressure.

The Interventionist asks the AI what would help him/her to feel less pressured at this time. S/he needs to know that if s/he makes a suicide threat, a 24-hour safety watch will be implemented immediately and the crisis hot line will be called if necessary. When the AI knows that specific consequences will be implemented when necessary, s/he is likely to feel supported by the Intervention Network.

The Interventionist also needs to prepare the Network for possible situations in which they may need to call the police. Intervention Network members need to be assured that if an emergency situation arises, they should not hesitate to call the police and/or the Interventionist, as saving the person's life is more important than any legal ramifications. Once the intensity of the ARISE Intervention process has been initiated, it is essential that the Interventionist, or a back-up person, be available at all times. Similarly, if the AI is in withdrawal from substance use, dangerous or life-threatening physical symptoms could result and the Network should be prepared to take him/her to the emergency room if this occurs.

The Interventionist explains to everyone how critical it is to clear the house of alcohol and other substances. Members are instructed to ask the addicted individual where s/he keeps his/her stash. The authors suggest providing ideas of possible hiding places other addicted individuals have used which include, but are not limited to, kitchen cabinets, freezers, curtain seams, dropped ceilings, chandeliers, toilet tanks, toilet rolls, basements, garages, car trunks, under mattresses, behind dressers, and in shoes, cereal boxes, make up containers and toothpaste tubes.

The Intervention Network must be prepared for the possibility that the AI might disappear in response to this Intervention. They should be forewarned and brainstorm locations that the addicted individual might run to and use as hideouts. The police should be called if this occurs. It is important to validate their fears and sense of powerlessness as these topics are addressed. Throughout the entire process, the Interventionist helps Network members prepare to use each other's supports for any situation or crisis that might arise.

The Interventionist works with Intervention Network members to identify the responsibilities of each Network member by asking the following questions: "Who will take the addicted individual's money if s/he is trying to buy drugs?" "Who will accompany him/her to the next meeting or to the treatment center?" "Who will remove weapons from the house?" The question of weapons is a particularly difficult and critical task and should be completed prior to the beginning of the Intervention (see the First Call worksheet, Appendix A) whenever possible, and certainly prior to the institution of any tough boundary-setting and consequences. If the AI is not present in this meeting, the ARISE Interventionist asks a member of the Intervention Network to contact him/her to discuss each of the options that were discussed in the meeting.

In summary, the Interventionist and the Intervention Network need to formulate plans for how to deal with each of the possibilities that have been raised. If there were a crisis, the Intervention Network will respond with competence knowing that everyone's safety has been planned for. This planning process ensures that the Intervention Network involves as many members as possible. No one person need feel alone and totally responsible. In the past, the person closest to the situation, typically the CO/Family Link had decided to "go it alone," and had reached the point of being overwhelmed and desperate, and determined to change the untenable situation, leading to the call to the ARISE Interventionist. The team approach inherent in the ARISE model promotes a positive outcome: the addicted individual engages in treatment.

DR. JUDITH LANDAU AND JAMES GARRETT

CHAPTER 9
Level II: Continued Further Level II Meetings

Objectives, Details and Tasks Specific to Subsequent Meetings

The process and flow of subsequent meetings follow the same pattern and the same focus: Substance use is not acceptable; the goal is to motivate the addicted individual (AI) to enter treatment; and there is an emphasis on Intervention Network consensus. Each of these subsequent meetings is conducted similarly to the first Level II meeting, including an update of the same basic objectives and tasks.

The Invitational Interventionist must be meticulous about following up on all tasks that have been assigned by the Intervention Network. S/he should also recognize previous disagreements, coalitions, and alliances, to ensure that these issues have been, or will be resolved, in subsequent meetings, while monitoring the AI's response to the Recovery Message. Continued encouragement is essential, especially when the AI fails to attend meetings.

Methods and Techniques

There will invariably be times when a member of the Intervention Network becomes angry, feels frustrated, threatens to withdraw, or falls back into old patterns of behavior relating to the addicted individual, perhaps even rejecting him/her. When each network member's perceptions of the situation are acknowledged and explored, the Interventionist works with these complications in order to continue building a stronger network of family recovery, whether or not the AI participates in the process. Openly addressing discouragement and a reluctance to continue the process will prevent the Intervention Network from falling into old patterns that would inevitably stymie the entire process.

Encouraging and supportive, the Interventionist helps Network members avoid burnout by preventing their taking on too much in the beginning and by reminding them that the treatment engagement process may take a long time. The Interventionist has to be available for trouble-shooting. If the Interventionist is unavailable for a time, arrangements for a back-up Interventionist are needed as events can move quickly and email or telephone contact can become critical.

Subsequent Level II sessions are marked by the ongoing development of new strategies to motivate the addicted individual to enter treatment. Typically, the Intervention Network agrees on a set of common responses to the AI to be used whenever there is contact between meetings. Examples might include, "We continue to worry about you. Will you consider coming to the next meeting?" or "You must feel embarrassed by our meeting to help you. What would work for you? I will tell the group what you would like from us."

These uniform responses, coming from all of the members of the Intervention Network as a "singular voice," accomplish several goals. Firstly, the group is unified and refuses to argue one-on-one with the AI. Secondly, the AI continues to be invited to be a part of the problem solving. Thirdly, ongoing contact among Intervention Network members and the AI between meetings maintains a single purpose—that of underlining the significance and seriousness of the problem. Fourthly, a message is conveyed to the AI that the group is committed to the process and will not give up no matter how long or difficult the process.

When the above focused messages are conveyed week after week to the AI, much information is collected regarding his/her readiness and barriers to change. New options may arise which will need to be discussed and negotiated. Continued meetings and ongoing communication with him/her illustrate the chronic nature of addiction putting time on the side of the Intervention Network.

The longer the process goes on, the more likely it is that the AI will experience additional problems relating to loss of control. If another problem does occur, its onset provides a new motivational opportunity for both the Intervention Network and the AI to support starting treatment. This process also bolsters the confidence and commitment of the Intervention Network to develop more stringent consequences if the AI does remain resistant to entering treatment.

If after two to five sessions, the addicted individual has still not attended a session, or is not willing to enter treatment, it becomes necessary to explore whether to proceed to Level III. The authors find it useful to have this discussion with the Intervention Network at each meeting subsequent to the first meeting. However, they rarely find it necessary to proceed to the formal ARISE Intervention and, in fact, do so in less than 2% of their cases.

The Transition from Level II to Level III

The following section describes the process of transitioning from Level II to Level III if, despite efforts made by the Intervention Network, the addicted individual has not come into treatment. The Intervention Network goes through a very careful process of discussion and decision-making about whether to proceed with a formal ARISE Intervention or to choose an alternative option. The goals for this transitional process are to guide the Intervention Network members to make a decision about the level of confrontation they are willing to employ, and finalize an action plan that matches the Intervention Network decision.

Bridging From Strength-in-Numbers to the Formal ARISE Intervention

Help the Intervention Network Reach a Decision:
Factors Influencing the Decision: Realizations that Need to be Reached and Actions that Need to be Taken

The addicted individual has difficulty making rational choices. During the decision-making process, it is helpful to point out to the Intervention Network that the AI's disease makes it almost impossible for him/her to make rational choices, especially when under the influence. The AI is caught in a downward, addictive spiral, which may result in his/her death. The AI needs the Intervention Network's help since his/her ability to make decisions has been severely compromised. The Intervention process is *not* what would cause the harm.

Shifting the focus from the addicted individual to the Intervention Network. Any logical decisions will necessarily be made by the Intervention Network and not by the AI; therefore, the focus is shifted from the AI to the Intervention Network. The Interventionist once again leads a discussion acknowledging the relationship patterns that develop from living with an actively addicted person, pointing out how difficult it is to change these patterns. Together the group can explore new ways for the network to build and maintain positive connections regardless of the AI's behavior. The Interventionist can remind them of their commitment that if the AI becomes suicidal or homicidal, they will immediately take him/her to an emergency department, or call the police. Throughout this process, the Interventionist encourages the Network to stay united, letting them know that, as they increase their efforts, the AI will also increase his/her efforts to divide and isolate them.

Drug use is not acceptable. During this time, it is critical for the Intervention Network to recognize that drug use is not acceptable. The Interventionist reminds them to maintain their decision to present a unified front, regardless of the AI's behavior. S/he makes it clear that the Network wants to get their loved one back—without the drug use. Network members realize that positive network relationships will continue regardless of the AI's decision.

At this stage, the Interventionist's most important task is to guide members of the Intervention Network toward making a firm commitment—both to each other and to the AI—to consistently acknowledge that he/she has a choice: either to have the network's love and support, or to continue the drug use. Members need to be encouraged to continue to support each other when consequences must be enforced. It is helpful to identify "susceptible" members who may be more vulnerable to pressure from the AI. Have the network develop a plan for staying united against such pressures and providing extra support for them. Be specific.

Reinforce benefit to the Intervention Network, whether or not the addicted individual gets well. The Interventionist helps members of the Intervention Network identify the positive aspects of setting limits and maintaining consequences. Network members' lives will continue to move in a forward direction, even if the AI keeps using drugs. The Interventionist reviews the natural history of addiction with the network, and helps members talk about potential losses and negative outcomes such as the medical, social, psychological, financial, legal, and occupational consequences, including the possible loss or death of the AI.

Test for Intervention Network consensus. The Interventionist facilitates a discussion about the members' fears and ambivalence, helping the

Intervention Network clarify the potential risks to themselves and to the AI in doing or not doing an ARISE Intervention. S/he helps network members support each other with the decision they have made, planning its implementation.

Put the Intervention Network Decision Into Action. This discussion begins with the particular choice that the family has made, remembering that this is a fluid process. The Interventionist helps the Intervention Network members explore their choice thoroughly, while supporting them in their deliberations. When the Network reaches a clear and firm decision, the Interventionist then works with the Network on the next step of action planning.

Shift the Power from the Addiction to the Intervention Network

The Interventionist will continue to discuss the possible choices that can be made by the Intervention Network at every Level II meeting. It is at this time that the Intervention Network is most likely to become aware that in order to take charge of the problem and find a solution, they will need to find a way to shift the power away from the disease of addiction and the AI. Ultimately, the Intervention Network will need to make final choices regarding the future functioning of the group. Final choices that the ARISE Interventionist needs to make patently clear to the Intervention Network members include:

"Maintain Status Quo." The first of these choices is to "maintain the status quo," which would mean that the Intervention Network would stop meeting and essentially stop the process of attempting to motivate the addicted AI to get into treatment. If they choose this decision, the Interventionist needs to be very certain that they truly understand their decision not to continue at this time and to communicate his/her acceptance of their decision. S/he can predict future problems for the addicted individual and offer an open invitation to the Network should things worsen.

Monitor the Process. The next alternative is to offer the Intervention Network the opportunity to monitor the process and be prepared to act when things inevitably get worse. This allows the Intervention Network an opportunity to take a "step back" and let things take their natural course. It is helpful for the Interventionist to bring up possible scenarios for what to do in the next crisis.

Introduce Consequences. The third alternative is to identify consequences while the Intervention Network monitors the process. Consequences are put in place that are immediate and concrete: e.g., taking away driving privileges, or requiring the addicted individual to be in treatment in order to remain living in the family home.

Proceed to Formal ARISE Intervention. The final choice is to proceed to a formal ARISE Intervention. The Invitational Interventionist helps the Intervention Network members support each other in taking this risk. Network members are encouraged to discuss their hopes and fears, and revisit the tasks of prior meetings to reassure themselves that they are indeed making the right decision. They are also strongly encouraged to make specific plans so that they are all completely aware of how to best deal with any eventuality.

The Final Level II Intervention Network Meeting:

If the Network decides to proceed to Level III, the following and final Level II meeting is conducted as follows:

Update Information. Early in the meeting, Intervention Network members who have had contact with the AI since the last session are asked to provide details about the nature of that contact. In this way, all of the Network members will be working with the same information about the AI. The Interventionist asks for specific information about the AI's responses, with particular attention to denial, rationalization, minimization, and projected blame. S/he gently helps network members understand how the AI might not be capable of making healthy decisions on his/her own, and that rational thinking cannot return without abstinence from drugs. In instances where there may be the complication of dual diagnosis, this is even more applicable.

Reviewing Past Attempts at Treatment Engagement. The Interventionist then rigorously reviews all past attempts made by the Intervention Network to get the AI to attend previous sessions. S/he inquires as to who invited him/her to attend and what the AI's reaction was to each invitation. The Interventionist validates the network's experience of loss due to the changes in the AI, and discusses how relationships across the network have been altered, both by the addiction and subsequently by the work of the Invitational Intervention.

Reviewing Attempts at Limit Setting. The Intervention Network then reviews how they have been setting limits with the AI and which attempts have succeeded and which have failed. They try to understand how the Network's limit setting with the AI has changed. For example, how are members dealing with such things as requests for money, the loan of a car, or absences from work?

Reinforcing the "Strength in Numbers" Approach. The Interventionist encourages Intervention Network members to support each other in their new limit-setting behaviors and preparation for the AI's likely response to changes in network members' behavior. At this stage, the emphasis is on the idea of "progress, not perfection." One of the most important decisions at this time is to make a commitment to maintaining family routines and rituals despite the temptation to live in a state of crisis.

The idea of the "strength in numbers" approach is reinforced and the Interventionist predicts that the AI may try to deal with one or more of the network members individually in an attempt to regain the "one-on-one" control that worked so well before the Intervention Network was formed.

DR. JUDITH LANDAU AND JAMES GARRETT

CHAPTER 10
Level III: The Formal ARISE Intervention

By the time the option of proceeding to Level III, the formal ARISE Intervention, is considered, the Interventionist typically has met with the Intervention Network three to five times in Level II sessions, in addition to the First Meeting in Level I. The Intervention Network has not yet been able to accomplish its goal of getting the addicted individual into treatment. At this stage of the process, the Intervention Network is left with few choices.

Logic would dictate that the consequences for not entering treatment would become more serious in order to match the resistance of the addicted individual (AI). This systematic progression of meetings, invitations, reaching out, support, and commitment to Family Motivation to Change justifies the implementation of more serious consequences. Therefore, by this time in the ARISE process, the Intervention Network decides to proceed to a more formal ARISE Intervention.

Finalizing the New Consequence

The task of the Interventionist now is to work with the Intervention Network to finalize what new and more serious consequences will be implemented if the AI does not enter treatment. There have likely been previous consequences set in motion from Level II sessions, so the consequences for Level III need to have a more serious impact. It is important that the entire Intervention Network support these new consequences due to the increased stakes. Following are examples of Level III consequences:

Parent consequence to adult child: "We will no longer tolerate your abusive behavior, nor continue to be the target of your anger and blame. If you choose not go into treatment after this meeting, you will not be invited to our home for any family functions. Please know, that we are serious and absolutely committed to getting our son back. You have our love and support. We hope you choose to enter treatment."

Adult child consequence to parent: "Your drinking in front of the grandchildren is not acceptable. We can no longer trust when you tell us that you have not been drinking when, in fact, you have. We will not risk the grandchildren's lives by leaving them alone with you under any circumstance.

If you do not enter treatment immediately, you will not see your grandchildren again. No more birthdays, school functions, babysitting, or having them over to your house. We will have to tell them that their grandfather is sick because he drinks too much and, until he gets treatment, they are not safe being with him. You know this breaks our hearts. The grandchildren love you and will miss you. Please make the right decision."

Spouse consequence to partner: "I don't know who I am living with any more. You have changed so much for the worse over the past few years. I have thought long and hard about what I am about to tell you. Please know that this is not an idle threat. If you don't get into treatment immediately, I will call a divorce attorney on Monday.

I cannot live like this any more. You are no longer the person I married. Your drug and alcohol use has destroyed our dreams and the love we once shared. Please know that I love you still and long for the person I married or I wouldn't be doing this. I would just let you destroy yourself and I would walk away. Please get help so that we can have our dreams together again."

Parent's consequence to an adolescent: "Your abusive attitude and disrespect, the stealing and legal problems and, most recently, your getting suspended from school are all clear messages that what we have been doing is not working. We will let the court decide your future if you do not go into treatment immediately. We will no longer pay for your attorney, and will let your Probation Officer know what is really going on in our house.

You have two weeks to find another place to live. Since Grandma is part of our decision-making staying with her is no longer an option. You may think this is harsh and we understand that you probably hate us right now, but all of this is a small price to pay to get our son/daughter back. These are not threats. Please make the right decision and accept our help."

Sibling consequence to a sibling: "We have been meeting as a group for the past couple of months trying to figure out how to reach you and get you help. We want you to know that we appreciated the two meetings you attended and the effort you made to try to beat your addiction problem. However, we have learned from the meetings that 'half-measures' just won't work. It is now time for you to get into that residential treatment program we talked about.

We made arrangements for you to check into the program right now. We will drive you there now and bring your clothes tomorrow. If you choose not to go we will change how we have contact with you. After the 4th of July picnic debacle where there were heated arguments that led to fighting, we have decided to no longer subject our family to those behaviors. Your outbursts create too much emotional wreckage to clean up. If you do not immediately enter treatment, you will no longer be invited to any family functions. Please get the help you need. Let's not let this disease tear up our family anymore."

The above examples demonstrate how severe the consequences need to be, how they logically fit specific past efforts, how the entire Intervention Network supports them, and how quickly they need to be implemented. The Interventionist needs regularly to remind the group that they would not be at this place if the addicted individual had accepted previous efforts. Because the consequences increase in severity and reach a bottom-line in Level III, the Interventionist must discuss consequences at the beginning of the Level III meetings.

The Intervention Network must be one hundred percent behind all consequences in order to move forward in planning the Formal ARISE Intervention. Having these discussions at the beginning of Level III has the added benefit of placing, front and center, the topic of how the individual members of the Intervention Network must take care of themselves both during the formal ARISE Intervention and afterwards.

It is useful to remind the Intervention Network that their feelings of guilt, shame, and blame, as well as other long-term stressors experienced by years of living with addiction have undoubtedly affected each and every one of the Network members individually. Thus, moving forward with the ARISE Intervention process is potentially of benefit to each of them, whether or not the AI eventually enters treatment.

The next sections of this chapter focus on practical steps the Interventionist follows for the preparation and implementation of the Formal ARISE Intervention.

Description of Preparatory Meetings Leading Up to the Formal Arise Intervention

Explain the "rehearsed nature" of the Intervention.

To a great extent, a Level III Intervention is a staged activity. Deliberate steps are followed to minimize surprise and to convey accurately and without distraction the consequences that the addicted individual will face if treatment is not accepted.

Discuss the Treatment options to be Presented Without Negotiation to the Addicted Individual.

The Interventionist will have previously reviewed with the group the various levels of care, payments, insurance coverage, and logistics for entering a treatment facility. This information determines the level of treatment the group is willing to accept. Then the Intervention Network plans for a certain outcome, such as inpatient rehabilitation, and holds firm to that plan during the Intervention meeting with the AI. During Levels I and II the Intervention Network is expected to enter into negotiations with the AI: The options are not negotiable in Level III.

Prepare the Intervention Network for the Intensity Often Experienced During a Level III ARISE Intervention.

The Formal ARISE Intervention is typically a short and to-the-point meeting lasting no longer than 45 minutes to one hour. The consequences are laid out and there is no room for negotiation. Very brief discussion may be allowed.

The Interventionist prepares the Intervention Network for the possibility of strong emotions. Network members are instructed to follow the steps as rehearsed with little discussion between members in order to avoid arguments and discord. At this stage it is important to remain united and avoid confrontation with the AI. Remind the group to remain supportive of one other, while maintaining regular contact following the ARISE Intervention, whether or not the AI enters treatment.

If the AI does enter treatment, the ARISE model encourages the members of the Intervention Network to become part of the treatment, perhaps having meetings at the treatment site itself. The Intervention Network transitions from its confrontational role to one of supporting the AI in recovery. They transition into becoming a Recovery Network.

If the addicted individual does not enter treatment, the Intervention Network agrees to meet for a determined number of future sessions to support each other in the implementation of the consequences. One of the key components of the follow-up meetings is to have an agreed upon plan that includes a quick response to the AI's reaching out for help in the future. This dynamic is highly probable given the predictable progression of negative consequences in the AI's life likely to lead to the eventuality of his/her "hitting bottom."

Following the Level III consensus building steps outlined above, the Interventionist now proceeds to work with the Intervention Network in preparation for a Formal ARISE Intervention.

Formal ARISE Intervention Preparation: Logistics
Decide Whom Will Participate.

The Interventionist helps the Intervention Network decide which members will participate. There may be reluctance by some individuals once the consequences have been agreed upon. It is important to coach the group toward inclusiveness. If one or more individuals drop out at this time, it is likely that the AI will see them as "weak links" and focus on them in the future to avoid treatment.

Write Letters.

The Interventionist instructs each network member to write a letter (to bring to the meeting), which will be read at the Intervention meeting. The letters contain the following elements: a statement of love and support for the AI; a listing of three-to five-specific instances of the AI's problem behavior related to alcohol and/or drug use and how it has affected the network member; a statement of the consequences developed by the group, and a request that the addicted individual get into treatment. Remind each member that the letters are to be kept as factual as possible. It may be helpful for the Interventionist to give the group members a sample letter to be used as a guide. (See sample letters in Appendix B).

Review Letters.

Ask the group to bring their letters to the next meeting. Have each network member read his/her letter while the others listen and then give constructive feedback on any items that sound angry, resentful, or judgmental. Have each person make the suggested revisions and re-read if necessary.

Role Play the Formal ARISE Intervention.

The Intervention Network decides on the order in which the letters will be read, typically placing the most powerful letters at the beginning and the end. The Interventionist describes his/her role in the Formal ARISE Intervention: S/he will begin the open the meeting with a request to the AI to listen to each person and then to respond only after everyone has spoken.

The following ground rules are established and agreed upon. There will be no physical violence or emotional abuse. Network members are not to engage in conversational disagreements with one another or with the AI once the meeting has started. Seating arrangements are made and other roles for Network members are defined, such as who would go outside with the AI if s/he leaves the room.

Have someone volunteer to play the role of the AI. The Interventionist is acting in role as well. Everyone then gets into their role and proceeds to role-play the ARISE Intervention. If possible, an audio or videotape of the role-play can be made for later critique. Formal ARISE Intervention sessions, including the role-play, are often emotion filled and Intervention Network members should be prepared for tears, joy, frustration, or any other emotion that arises.

Finalize Logistics.

The network decides on the date, time, and place for the Formal ARISE Intervention meeting. When possible, treatment arrangements are prearranged. Managed care and insurance pre-certification are completed after the role-play meeting and before the actual Intervention meeting. An invitation is again extended to the AI to attend this meeting. The invitation differs, however, in that the s/he is now requested to attend this one meeting only. If s/he is not willing to meet, then one or more of the Intervention Network members takes the letters to the AI's home to be read to him/her there. The Interventionist may or may not accompany the group, but is available by phone to check-in and to deal with any consequences.

Set Up a Plan to Deal With Any New Problem With the Addicted Individual

The Interventionist helps the network prepare for a possible crisis, which may occur between the final preparation meeting and the time of the Formal Intervention meeting. The Interventionist assures the members that s/he is available during this interim time to provide support and help with any feelings of concern and anxiety.

Discuss the Need for the Network Members to Support Each Other.

Remind the members of the group that they have agreed on a consequence that most likely previously has not been enforced. Therefore, it is normal to have second thoughts and doubt whether or not this is the right thing to do. Encourage continued regular contact and support for one another. This is also a good time to reinforce that individuals attend self-help meetings, such as Al-Anon.

The Formal ARISE Intervention

The following steps are followed at the Intervention meeting:

Introduction

The Interventionist introduces him/herself, briefly states the purpose of the meeting, and asks if the AI is willing to listen to what each person has to say before responding.

Read Letters

Each network member reads the letter s/he has written, being careful not to deviate from, or to add to, the letter. If the AI makes any comments following each reading they would briefly be addressed at this time.

Addicted Individual's Decision

After the last letter is read, all remain silent. This silence provides time for the AI to respond, but it can also serve to heighten tension and the intensity of the upcoming decision by the AI. If s/he does not break the silence with a response, the Interventionist thanks the group and turns to him/her asking, "Are you ready to start treatment?"

Discuss Treatment Options

The Interventionist reiterates what the Intervention Network had requested and discusses available levels of care. Often the AI will want clarification on what "starting treatment" means. There may be a period of discussion about treatment options, but if the s/he does not agree to treatment after 15-20 minutes of discussion, the Interventionist calls an end to the session, restates the agreed upon consequences to everyone and notifies everyone when the group has agreed to meet again.

If the AI agrees to start treatment, the Interventionist invites the Intervention Network members to offer congratulations and sets in motion the logistics to start treatment, for instance, going to a hospital detoxification program or making a call to get started in an outpatient program.

Set Up a Plan to Deal with Decisions Made During the Session

If the AI agrees to enter treatment, the Intervention Network plans to do one or a combination of the following (depending on the level of care decided on): drive him/her to the rehabilitation center; ask about accompanying him/her to the initial intake session at outpatient; ask permission to help with removing alcohol and other drugs from the house; discuss alternative living arrangements that are supportive of early recovery, knowing how difficult the next four-to-six weeks are likely to be; and attend self-help meetings with the addicted individual.

Discuss the Need for Network Members to Support Each Other Until the Next Meeting

Remind the group that the network will continue to meet as a Recovery Network after the Formal ARISE Intervention session as long as group members feel the need for support. These meetings are held to support the addicted individual who has entered treatment and/or to support one another in the implementation of the consequences. Emphasis is placed on the idea that an ARISE Intervention is a process continuing as long as the group benefits from the support.

In summary, the ARISE Intervention is a win-win situation. On the one hand, the AI will enter treatment. On the other hand, the family has united in support of him/her and relinquished feelings such as blame, shame, and anger. Because the Intervention Network established new and more serious consequences, a powerful statement is made that addiction no longer controls family interactions.

PART III
EXPANDED APPLICATION OF ARISE

DR. JUDITH LANDAU AND JAMES GARRETT

CHAPTER 11
Applying ARISE to Other Behavioral Problems

I nvitational Intervention and the ARISE protocols can be applied to a number of non-substance related addictions and dependencies that are often as disruptive to individual and family life as substance abuse. These tend to fall into three main categories: (a) Other addictions and behavioral compulsions, (b) chronic and/or life-threatening physical or psychiatric disorders, and (c) physical or emotional problems that threaten primary relationships but are not severe enough to warrant psychiatric referral.

Other Addictions and Behavioral Compulsions:

Dependence on pain medication/prescription drugs
Gambling
Workaholism
Sexual Addiction
Nicotine Dependence
Internet Addiction—games, gambling
Compulsive Spending
Eating Disorder—anorexia, bulimia, binging, chocolate dependence, sugar dependence
Obesity

Chronic and/or Life-Threatening Psychiatric or Physical Disorders:
Physical:

Chronic illness: diabetes, asthma
Heart disease, hypertension
Chronic pain with medication dependence

Cancer
Behavior change due to thyroid disease or other endocrine disorders

Psychiatric:

Bipolar disease
Schizophrenia
Mood disorders: (particularly dual diagnosis; chronic depression and unresolved grief)
Anxiety disorders: (specifically PTSD, social anxiety and phobic disorders, separation anxiety)

Physical or Emotional Problems, Not Severe Enough to Warrant Psychiatric Referral, but Threaten Primary Relationships

Mild Traumatic Brain Injury
Chronic illness of any type that is not severe enough to require medical management but requires emotional or psychotherapeutic management
Chronic emotional disturbance

The authors have applied Invitational Intervention to all of the problems listed above and found the ARISE Intervention extremely effective at engaging resistant patients and clients in treatment, and ensuring that they maintain their treatment. An Intervention Network coached by an Invitational Interventionist can bring about a remarkable change when a patient resists regular testing of blood, urine, or blood pressure, does not attend doctor's appointments regularly, and is reluctant to comply with prescribed medication, to list just a few examples in one category.

When approached by a First Caller about any of these problems, the Invitational Interventionist proceeds in much the same way as s/he would in dealing with a substance abuse issue. However, in each of the categories and sub-categories there are likely to be differences, ranging from subtle to blatant. It is important to be aware of these differences and the need for specific training prior to offering one's services in any of these areas.

The first author, Dr. Landau, was for many years, a professor of psychiatry and family medicine, and it was during this time that both authors were able to develop and test the application of ARISE in medical specialty, primary care, and collaborative settings.

For the sake of brevity, the authors have decided to present only a few case vignettes in illustration. In subsequent pairs of books (each set comprising one for professionals and one for the lay public), they will elaborate on the specific application of Invitational Intervention to the categories and/or problems listed above. If the reader is interested in contacting the authors concerning any of these areas, they would be glad to receive communication at their website: www.LinkingHumanSystems.com.

The Case of Sara with Mild Traumatic Brain Injury (MTBI)

Sara was an intelligent, hard-working speech and language therapist who had been happily married for several years. While sitting at a stoplight one afternoon, Sara's vehicle was rear-ended. Treated only for whiplash in the emergency room, she was sent home unaware that any long-term damage had occurred. In the weeks following the accident, Sara began feeling depressed and anxious. She was unable to concentrate and function at work, and at home she was prone to emotional outbursts. Suffering from severe back and shoulder pain during the day, she would also wake in the middle of the night with clenched jaw and fists, and severe cramping in her feet and arms. A previously placid person, she started fights with people and afterwards could not remember what the disagreement had been about.

Sara's internist tried to persuade her to see a psychiatrist for her symptoms of chronic pain and post-traumatic stress disorder, but she resisted, insisting that there was nothing wrong with her except for the severe injuries sustained in the accident. Despite her doctor's pleading, and insistence that she could be helped to feel a great deal better, sleep through the night, and suffer less pain, Sara was adamant about not taking his advice. The situation progressively deteriorated. Sara and her husband

David were finding it impossible to communicate as they once had and marital stress increased. They constantly fought, and David asked Sara to reduce her work hours because he felt that the driving required by the geographic scatter of her clients was increasing her symptoms. Sara was experiencing increasing stress and anxiety when she drove, particularly in bad weather and at sunrise or sunset. She also suffered from severe headaches, and after a long day's work, would find that her vision was badly blurred. She would wake at night dreaming about accidents and be apprehensive about getting into the car the next day.

David, Sara's mother, her sister, and her internist all tried in vain to persuade her to call a psychiatrist. The internist finally called an ARISE Interventionist who guided him through the First Call. Because he was not a family member, the ARISE Interventionist encouraged him to invite a member of the family to serve as a Co-Family Link or Co-Concerned Other (CO). Sara's mother accepted the role, albeit reluctantly because she, along with David, had been bearing the brunt of Sara's extreme and unpredictable rages.

As mentioned earlier, Co-Links or Co-COs are commonly used. In cases where the First Caller is not a relative, or intimately familiar with the patient/client or family, the family often chooses a Co-CO from their own ranks. This situation commonly arises where the First Caller is a professional such as a social worker, an emergency room nurse, or a primary care physician or internist, as was the case here.

The Co-COs were able to mobilize Sara's husband, sister, father and best friend, although her father did not attend meetings. Unfortunately, by the time she did seek treatment for PTSD, the relationship with her husband had drastically deteriorated. Feelings of guilt, anger, rejection and resentment intensified in the marriage, and the change in her "sense of self" and David's view of her, further strained their relationship.

Sara, through the Intervention process, became more aware of the ways in which the MTBI had affected her life. She began to set more realistic goals for rehabilitation and felt hopeful that her marriage could be salvaged. However, after years of ongoing stress and conflict, David was unwilling to continue marriage counseling and filed for divorce believing that Sara had become a different person from the one he married.

This case illustrates how Invitational Intervention can be used to motivate someone with a physical and/or mental illness to enter treatment. Unfortunately, Sara's story is all too common in people with MTBI, a majority ending up in divorce courts. Had the ARISE Intervention method been used earlier, there was a good chance that her marriage might have been saved. The Intervention Network was able, however, to support Sara through the divorce and its aftermath, and she is now functioning well.

The Case of Jeff and Morbid Obesity

The ARISE Interventionist received the First Call from Jeff's wife, Marge, who stated that her husband collapsed over the weekend and was taken to the hospital and released the same day. The hospital staff informed her that her husband would die if he did not lose weight. Jeff refused to get help and told Marge in the car returning home that it was just the heat that caused him to lose consciousness. While completing the First Call worksheet, the Interventionist gathered significant information that would be used when conducting the Intervention. Jeff, age 49, was morbidly obese. He currently weighed 370 pounds and was 5'11" tall. He had suffered a serious car accident when he was 39 that resulted in a chronic pain condition from a spinal disc injury. This accident resulted in several losses, including the inability to continue training for triathlons, loss of flexibility in his lower back, and loss of ability to work full time until three years ago. His mother had been an alcoholic and his father had a history of compulsive gambling.

Jeff had never been a drinker "because of how turned off I was from my mother's drinking." He had no prior history of an eating disorder before the accident ten years ago. Jeff was married at age 26 and has three children, ages 14, 11 and 8. He works in a middle-management position for a large insurance company. He began competing in triathlons three years before the car accident and was active in the local triathlon club. His training weight when he was competing was 180 pounds. His current health problems included chronic back pain, loss of lower back mobility, high blood pressure, sleep apnea and pre-diabetic symptoms.

The ARISE Interventionist and Jeff's wife agreed that the Intervention Network would include the following: Jeff's older brother and younger sister (who would come in from out of town), Marge's two younger siblings (who lived in the area), two members of their church, and three friends from Jeff's triathlon days. Marge decided not to involve the children at this point, but was open to involving them in future meetings. It was agreed that the best place to meet would be at Jeff and Marge's home. The Intervention Network members were invited, as was Jeff. He initially protested and threatened not to come to the meeting, but after an encouraging call from one brother agreed to come to "only one" meeting.

The First Call meeting started with each of the individuals giving Jeff a hug and thanking him for the courage it took to attend. Most of those present did not think he would show up. Each of the Intervention Network members shared their love for Jeff and their growing concerns over his large weight gain, especially over the past four years, when he had gained 150 pounds. The conglomeration of family, friends, and athletes who used to train and compete with Jeff provided an interesting mix of stories, concern and support.

Jeff responded somewhat defensively to the issues of obesity and health deterioration when in the middle of a sentence he stopped, teared up as he looked at his older brother and said, "I just remembered how scared I was when the ambulance came that time when I was 15 and took Mom away after she fell down the stairs drunk. Do you remember that? God, I don't want my kids to feel that way about me. They probably do after what happened a couple of weekends ago."

Jeff's spontaneous openness led to the group discussing various treatment options including: gastric bypass surgery, residential treatment for eating disorders, outpatient treatment, a dietician consultation, and/or a full medical examination. Jeff agreed to start with a complete medical exam, something he had been avoiding the past two years. He agreed to allow his wife to go with him and to present the results when the group next met. At the next meeting, Jeff reported on his medical condition. He learned he had diabetes, an enlarged heart, high blood pressure, and degenerative discs in his spine, mostly due to his obesity. He was referred to a local physician who specialized in eating disorders and obesity to begin a regimen of diet and moderate exercise. The main source of weight gain was from sugar, with Jeff reporting that he would often eat (mostly sneaking the food) a bag of cookies, a dozen candy bars and up to a gallon of ice cream a day. With this in mind, the group came up with the idea of "working a recovery" program with the "sobriety" goal of abstinence from eating sugar and doing it one-day-at-a-time. Jeff agreed to accept a daily phone call from one of the Intervention Network members to reinforce his commitment. He also committed to start attending 12 Step meetings in the area with one of the group members who was a member of his church.

Jeff went through "withdrawal" symptoms similar to those reported by addicts who stop using drugs. For the first month of "sobriety" Jeff reported the following symptoms: daily cravings that lasted for 5-10 minutes and occurred at least six times a day; physical shaking; sweating; daily headaches; stomach cramping, leg muscle cramping, difficulty concentrating, urges to sneak eat, lying about food, triggers to binge given that he had money in his wallet, and frequent "binging" dreams. Jeff reported, "I could totally identify with what I heard at AA meetings, except for me it was about sugar, not alcohol. Otherwise, it was almost exactly the same."

The Intervention Network met twice a month for the first three months and then once a month for the next six months. During that nine-month period, Jeff "relapsed" three times, but each time used the experience to strengthen his goal of recovery. He accomplished the following: a stable diabetic condition that did not require medication, lowered blood pressure (with medication), weight loss of 30 pounds, start of moderate exercise, regular attendance at 12 Step meetings, work with a 12-Step sponsor, and the acceptance of recognizing his binge eating as an addiction.

On a psychological-emotional level, Jeff began to work with a therapist on issues related to loss connected to his mother and her alcoholism; loss of his father to compulsive gambling; and loss of his athletic body due to the car accident. Jeff reported that the work on grief and loss was an important part of his "recovery" due to his use of sugar to escape from "the pain I never wanted to face, but just kept eating at me."

This is an example of an ARISE case that successfully used an Invitational Intervention to help with an eating disorder. It also demonstrates how the model of addiction and recovery can be applied to problems other than alcohol or drug addiction. As the case progressed, the relapse prevention plan evolved around the loss work. This type of psychotherapy is important, if not necessary, because if the eating was "but a symptom of the underlying problem", then the underlying problem(s) must be addressed or a relapse would occur to numb the unresolved pain. The self-medicating use of drugs and alternative addictions needs to be addressed, and this can best be achieved in therapy, preferably in an extended family setting, as was the case with Jeff. His story also shows how appropriate medical professionals are necessary to address the sequalae or secondary results of obesity. A strong collaborative team is a necessity for good results in a situation like this one.

Both Jeff and Amy were able to regain control of their lives despite having suffered major disruptions. Those close to them had observed their problems and found a professional who helped them intervene with the formation of an Intervention Network. The ARISE method is successful no matter what the problem or underlying cause; the key ingredient in both stories is that the family became motivated to change. The ARISE method builds on the strengths and commitment of this support network. The authors' research has shown that most individuals in need of help are willing to participate in a family meeting centered around the topic of their use when a loving and direct approach is used to invite them. Even Amy, who did not believe that there was anything wrong with her, entered treatment after she realized how concerned her support Network was.

The ARISE method of Invitational Intervention is useful in many more situations than just alcohol and drug addiction concerns. As the case of Jeff teaches, getting the individual into treatment and supporting them long-term can heal a family and prevent the addiction from being passed on to future generations.

Judith Landau, MD, DPM, CFLE

Dr. Landau, child, family and community psychiatrist, formerly Professor of Psychiatry and Family Medicine at the University of Rochester, is President of Linking Human Systems, LLC, a global training and consulting business, and Director of the Recovery Resource Center, Boulder, CO. She currently serves as Consultant on Addiction to the Kosova Government and has consulted to the governments of several other countries after trauma and disaster resulting in increased addiction rates, including Argentina, Hungary, and Taiwan. She has taught in over 90 countries and written a book and over 150 chapters and articles on the theory and background research of Invitational Intervention™ and Family Motivation to Change® including articles on the ARISE method and outcome studies. Dr. Landau was the Principal Investigator on the NIDA-funded research study of ARISE. She also facilitates Interventions throughout the United States.

James Garrett, LCSW

Mr. Garrett is Vice-President of Linking Human Systems, LLC, a global training and consulting business. He is also Director of the Recovery Resource Center, Albany, NY. He has participated in over 500 Interventions and has provided Intervention training to treatment providers in the US and other countries including Hungary, Belgium and Kosova. Mr. Garrett is the principal author of 5 peer-reviewed journal articles on Intervention and has co-authored another 5 additional articles related to treatment outcomes and Intervention. He was a Co-Investigator on the NIDA-funded research study on ARISE. He conducts ARISE training programs for both individual agencies and community groups. He also facilitates Interventions throughout the United States.

This book has led the reader "Step by Step" through the ARISE method of conducting Invitational Interventions. Its authors, Jim and Judith, as well as their hard working colleagues, tested the protocol through a research project funded by the National Institute on Drug Abuse (NIDA RO1 DA09402).

The subsequent development of Invitational Intervention and other protocols that grew from Transitional Family Theory and Therapy and their belief in the inherent resilience in individuals, families and communities, led Judith and Jim to believe that these methods should be made available to individuals, families, and communities around the world. Judith, therefore, took early retirement from her academic position as professor of psychiatry and family medicine and as Director of the Division of Family Programs at the University of Rochester, so that they could actualize their dream.

Next, Jim and Judith created Linking Human Systems, LLC, and LINC Foundation, Inc. to continue the development and implementation of their ideas and beliefs. Judith established the Recovery Resource Center in Boulder, Colorado, while Jim established the Recovery Resource Center in Albany, New York, Currently, both have private practices working with individuals and families using the ARISE method and the ARISE Invitational Intervention principles described in this book.

DR. JUDITH LANDAU AND JAMES GARRETT

INVITATIONAL INTERVENTION

Linking Human Systems (LHS) and LINC Foundation (LINC)

Mission Statement

We believe in the inherent resilience and competence of individuals, families and communities. Our mission is to mobilize this resource to aid in healing from past and present trauma and its consequences. LHS and LINC develop and provide resiliency based training and consultation that address the psychosocial, cultural, economic and spiritual rehabilitation of individuals, families and communities. They also provide consultation in maximizing performance based on resilience.

Specific attention is given to reaching vulnerable individuals, families and communities impacted by chronic and life-threatening physical and psychiatric illnesses including addiction, HIV/AIDS, psychosomatic problems, heart disease, cancer, and families dealing with the aftermath of trauma, suffering relational disintegration and violence, uprootedness and cultural transition, and recovery from human-made or natural disasters.

The Clinical and Training operations are based in Albany and Boulder at the Recovery Resource Centers.

For more information about Linking Human Systems, LLC please visit the websites: www.LinkingHumanSystems.com, www.RecoveryResourceCenter.com and www.LINC Foundation.info

Contact information:

Dr. Judith Landau
503 Kalmia Avenue
Boulder, Colorado 80304-1733

James Garrett
301 South Allen Street
Albany, New York 12208

303-442-3755
877-229-5462
Jlandau@linkinghumansystems.com

518-446-9191
Garrett@ linkinghumansystems.com

BIBLIOGRAPHY

Andreasen, N.C., Endicott, J., Reich, T., & Coyell, W. (1986). The family history approach to diagnosis: How useful is it? *Archives of General Psychiatry, 43,* 421-429.

Auerswald, E.H. (1968). Interdisciplinary versus Ecological approach. *Family Process, 7,* 202-215.

Barber, J.G. & Gilbertson, R. (1997). Unilateral interventions for women living with heavy drinkers. *Social Work, 42(1),* 69-77.

Barnes, G.M. (1990). Impact of the family on adolescent drinking patterns. In R.L. Collins, K.E. Leonard, & J.S. Searles (Eds.), *Alcohol and the family: Research and clinical perspectives.* New York: Guilford.

Black, C., Bucky, S.F., & Wilder-Padilla, S. (1986). The interpersonal and emotional consequences of being an adult child of an alcoholic. *International Journal of the Addictions, 21(2),* 213-231.

Boszormenyi-Nagy, I., & Spark, G. (1973). *Invisible loyalties: Reciprocity in intergenerational family therapy.* New York: Harper & Row.

Bowen, M. (1974). Alcoholism as viewed through family systems theory and family psychotherapy. *Annals of the New York Academy of Sciences, 233,* 115-122.

Bowen, M. (1978). Family therapy and clinical practice. New York: Jason Aronson.

Boyd, C.P., Gullone, E., Needleman, G.L., & Burt, T. (1997). The Family Environment Scale: Reliability and normative data for an adolescent sample. *Family Process, 36,* 369-373.

Bray, J.H., Maxwell, S.E., & Cole, D. (1995). Multivariate statistics for family Psychology research. *Journal of Family Psychology, 9,* 144-160.

Brim, O.G., & Ryff, C.D. (1980). On the properties of life events. In P.D. Bates & O.G. Brim (Eds.), *Life-span development and behavior (Vol. 3).* New York: Academic Press.

Brook, J.S., Brook, D.W., Gordon, A.S., Whiteman, M., & Cohen, P. (1990). The psychosocial etiology of adolescent drug use: A family interactional approach. *Genetic, Social, and General Psychology Monographs, 116,* 111-267.

Brown, D.H. (1993). Adolescents' perceptions of the essential therapeutic processes and treatment ingredients in an effective residential treatment program for emotionally disturbed adolescents: A grounded theory approach. *Dissertation Abstracts International, 53(8B),* 4365.

Brown, H.P., & Peterson, J.H. (1991). Assessing spirituality in addiction treatment and follow-up: Development of the Brown-Peterson Recovery Progress Inventory. *Alcoholism Treatment Quarterly, 8(2),* 21-50.

Brown, S.A. (1987). Alcohol use and type of life events experienced during adolescence. *Psychology of Addictive Behaviors, 1,* 104-107.

Brown, S.A., Mott, M.A., & Myers, M.G. (1990). Adolescent drug and alcohol treatment outcome. In R. R. Watson (Ed.), *Drug and alcohol abuse prevention* (pp. 373-403). Clifton, NJ: Humana Press.

Brown, S.A., Myers, M.G., Mott, M.A., & Vik, P.W. (1994). Correlates of success following treatment for adolescent substance abuse. *Applied and Preventive Psychology, 3,* 61-73.

Califano, J.A., It's drugs, stupid, *New York Times Magazine,* January 29, p. 41 (1995).

Coleman, S.B., & Stanton, M.D. (1979). The role of death in the addict family. *Journal of Marital and Family Counseling, 4,* 79-91.

Daley, D. C., Mercer, J.D., & Carpenter, G. (1998). *Group drug counseling manual.* Holmes Beach, FL: Learning Publications.

Fishman, H.C., Stanton, M.D., & Rosman, B.L. (1982). Treating families of adolescent drug abusers. In Stanton, M.D., Todd T.C., & Associates, *The family therapy of drug abuse and addiction* (pp. 335-357). NY: Guilford Press.

Framo, J.L. (1976). Family of origin as a therapeutic resource for adults in marital and family therapy: You can and should go home again. *Family Process, 15,* 193-210.

Frances, R.J., Miller, S.I., & Galanter, M. (1989). Psychosocial treatment of addictions. In A. Tasman, R.J. Hales & A. Frances (Eds.), *Review of psychiatry, Vol. 8;* pp. 341-359). Washington, DC: American Psychiatric Press.

Frone, M.R., Cooper, M.L., & Russell, M. (1994). Stressful life events, gender and substance use: An application of regression. *Psychology of Addictive ehaviors, 8(2),* 59-69.

Galanter, M. (1993). *Network therapy for alcohol and drug abuse.* New York: Basic Books.

Galanter, M., Castaneda, R., & Franco, H. (1991). Group therapy and self-help groups. In R.J. Frances, & S.I. Miller (Eds.), *Clinical textbook of addictive disorders.* New York: Guilford Press.

Garrett, J. & Landau, J. (In Press, 2006). *Invitational Intervention: A Step-By-Step Guide for Getting Your Loved One into Addiction Treatment.* www.BookSurgePublishing.com.

Garrett, J. & Landau, J. (In Press, 2006*). Invitational Intervention: A Step-By-Step Guide for Getting Your Loved One into Addiction Treatment.* Binghamton, NY: Haworth Press.

Garrett, J. & Landau, J. (In Press 2006). Family Motivation to Change: A major factor in engaging alcoholics in treatment. By invitation for special issue of *Alcohol Treatment Quarterly.*

Garrett, J., Landau-Stanton, J., Stanton, M.D., Baciewicz, G., Shea, R., Brinkman-Sull, D. (1996). *ARISE: A manual for engaging substance abusers in treatment, University of Rochester, (unpublished manual).*

Garrett, J., Landau-Stanton, J., Stanton, M.D., Baciewicz, G., Shea, R., Brinkman-Sull, D. (1998). The ARISE Intervention: Using family and network links to engage addicted persons in treatment. *Journal of Substance Abuse Treatment, 15(2),* 333-343.

Garrett, J., Landau-Stanton, J., Stanton, M.D., Baciewicz, G., Shea, R., Brinkman-Sull, D. (1999). The "Concerned Other" call: Using family links and networks to overcome resistance to addiction treatment. *Journal of Substance Use and Misuse, 34(3)* 363-382.

Garrett, J., Landau-Stanton, J., Stanton, M.D., Stellato-Kabat, J., & Stellato-Kabat, D. (1997). ARISE: A method for engaging reluctant alcohol- and drug-dependent individuals in treatment. *Journal of Substance Abuse Treatment, 14(3):* 235-248.

Gerstein, D.R., Johnson, R.A., Harwood, H.J., et al., *Evaluating Recovery Services: The California Drug and Alcohol Treatment Assessment (CALDATA).* Sacramento,

Grant, B.F., & Dawson, D.A. (1997). Age at onset of alcohol use and its association with DSM-IV alcohol dependence: Results of the National Longitudinal Alcohol Epidemiology Survey. *Journal of Substance Abuse, 9*, 103-110.

Haley, J. (1976). *Problem-solving therapy*. San Francisco: Jossey-Bass.

Haley, J. (1980). *Leaving home*. New York: McGraw-Hill.

Henggeler, S.W., Borduin, C.M., Melton, G.B., Mann, B.J., Smith, L.A., Hall, J.A., Cone, L., & Fucci, B.R. (1991). Effects of multisystemic therapy on drug use and abuse in serious juvenile offenders: A progress report from two outcome studies. *Family Dynamics of Addiction Quarterly, 1(3)*, 40-51.

Henggeler, S.W., Melton, G.B., Brondino, M.J., Scherer, D.G., & Hanley, J.H. (1997). Multisystemic therapy with violent and chronic juvenile offenders and their families: The role of treatment fidelity in successful dissemination. *Journal of Consulting and Clinical Psychology, 65(5)*.

Hill, C.E., O'Grady, K.E., Elkin, L. (1992). Applying the collaborative study psychotherapy rating scale to rate therapist adherence in cognitive-behavior therapy, interpersonal therapy, and clinical management. *Journal of Consulting and Clinical Psychology, 60, 73-79*.

Hogue, A., Liddle, H., Rowe, C., Turner, R., Dakof, G., & LaPann, K. (1998). Treatment adherence and differentiation in individual vs. family therapy for adolescent drug abuse. *Journal of Counseling Psychology, 45*, 104-114.

Hogue, A., Rowe, C., Liddle, H., & Turner, R. (1994). *Scoring manual for the Therapist Behavior Rating Scale (TBRS)*. Unpublished manuscript, Center for Research on Adolescent Drug Abuse, Temple University, Philadelphia, PA.

Imber-Black, E. (1988). *Families and larger systems: A family therapist's guide through the labyrinth*. New York: Guilford Press.

Inciardi, J.A. (1995). Crack, crack house sex, and HIV risk. *Archives of Sexual Behavior, 24(3)*, 249-269.

Johnson, V. (1986). *Intervention-How to help someone who doesn't want help*. Minneapolis: Johnson Institute Books.

Johnson, V. (1973). *I'll quit tomorrow*. New York: Harper & Row.

Kessler, R.C., McGonagle, K.A., Zhao, S., Nelson, C.B., Hughes, M., Eshleman, S., Wittchen, H-U., & Kendler, K.S. (1994). Lifetime and 12-month prevalence of DSM- III-R psychiatric disorders in the United States: Results from the National Comorbidity Survey. *Archives of General Psychiatry, 51*, 8-19.

Landau, J. (1981). Link therapy as a family therapy technique for transitional extended families. *Psychotherapeia, 7(4)*, 382-390.

Landau, J. (1982). Therapy with families in cultural transition. In M. McGoldrick, J.K. Pierce, & J. Giordano (Eds.), *Ethnicity and family therapy* (pp. 552-572). New York: Guilford Press.

Landau, J. (1986). Competence, impermanence and transitional mapping. In L. C. Wynne, S. H. McDaniel, & T. Weber, (Eds.), *Systems consultation: A new perspective for family therapy*. New York: Guilford Press.

Landau, J. (2004). El modelo LINC: una estrategia colaborativa para la resiliencia comunitaria. *Sistemas Familiares, 20 (3)*; (English Translation available; The LINC Model: A Collaborative Strategy for Community Resilience.) Published in digital format at www.e-libro.com.

format at www.e-libro.com.

Landau, J & Garrett, J. (In Press, 2006). *Invitational Intervention: A Step-by-Step Guide for Clinicians.* Binghamton, NY: Haworth Press.

Landau, J., & Griffiths, J.A. (1981). The extended family in transition: Clinical implications. *Psychotherapeia, 7(4),* 370-381. Republished in F. Kaslow (Ed.), *The international book of family therapy,* New York: Brunner/Mazel, 1982.

Landau, J. & Hissett, J.L. (In press, 2007). Mild Traumatic Brain Injury: Impact on Identity and Ambiguous Loss in the Family. *Family Relations, 56(2).*

Landau, J., & Saul, J. (2004). Facilitating family and community resilience in response to major disaster. In F. Walsh & M. McGoldrick (eds.), *Living Beyond Loss* (pp. 285-309). New York: Norton.

Landau, J., Shea, R.R., Garrett, J., Stanton, M.D., Brinkman-Sull, D., & Baciewicz, G. (1999). Strength in numbers: The ARISE method for using family and network to engage addicted persons in treatment. Manuscript submitted for publication.

Landau, J., & Stanton, M.D. (1983). Therapeutic intervention: Families with adolescent substance abusers. *Focus on Alcohol and Drug Issues, 6(3),* 2-3, 20.

Landau, J., & Stanton, M.D. (1998). A model for alcoholism and addiction within the family: I. Intergenerational genesis and the "When did it start?" question. Manuscript submitted for publication.

Landau, J., & Weaver, A. M. (In Press, 2006) The LINC Model of Community Resilience: Policy Implications for Disaster Preparedness, Response & Recovery. *Journal of Family & Consumer Sciences, Volume 98, Issue 2.*

Landau-Stanton, J. (1990). Issues and methods of treatment for families in cultural Transition. In M.P. Mirkin (Ed.), *The social and political contexts of family therapy.* Needham Heights, MA: Allyn and Bacon.

Landau-Stanton, J., Clements, C.D., & Associates (1993). *AIDS, health and mental health: A primary source book.* New York: Brunner/Mazel.

Landau-Stanton, J., Le Roux, P., Horwitz, S., Baldwin, S., & McDaniel, S. (1992). Grandma come help. In T.S. Nelson and S.S. Trepper (Eds.). *101 Favorite family therapy interventions.* Binghamton, NY: The Haworth Press.

Landau-Stanton, J. & Stanton, M.D. (1985). Treating suicidal adolescents and their families. In M.P. Mirkin and S.L Korman (Eds.), *Handbook of Adolescents and Family Therapy.* New York: Gardner Press.

Landau-Stanton, J., & Stanton, M.D. (1986). Family Therapy and systems supervision with the "Pick-a-Dali Circus model. In F.W. Kaslow (Ed.) *Supervision and Training Models, Dilemmas and Challenges.* New York: Haworth Press.

Liddle, H.A., Diamond, G.M., & Becker, D. (1997). Family therapy supervision. In C. Watkins (Ed.), *Psychotherapy supervision.* New York: Wiley Publishers.

Loneck, B., Garrett, J., & Banks, S. (1996a). A comparison of the Johnson Intervention with four other methods of referral to outpatient treatment. *The American Journal of Drug and Alcohol Abuse, 22(2),* 233-246.

Loneck, B., Garrett, J., & Banks, S. (1996b). The Johnson Intervention and relapse during outpatient treatment. *The American Journal of Drug and Alcohol Abuse, 22(3),* 363-375.

McDaniel, S. & Landau-Stanton, J. (1992). Family therapy skills training and family of Origin work: Both/And. *Family Process, 30:*459-471.

Mederer, H. & Hill, I. (1983). Critical transitions over the family lifespan: Theory and research. In H. I. McCubbin, M.B. Sussman, & J.M. Patterson (Eds.), *Social stress and the family*, (pp. 39-60). New York: Haworth Press.

Meyers, R.J., Smith, J.E., & Miller, E.J., (1998). Working through the concerned significant other: Community reinforcement and family training. In W.R. Miller & N. Heather (Eds.), *Treating addictive behaviors: Process of change (2nd edition)*. New York: Plenum Press.

Miller, W.R., & Myers, R.J. (1996). *Unilateral family intervention for drug problems: Stage II trial (NIDA grant No. RO1 DA –08896-01)*. Albuquerque: University of New Mexico, Center for Alcoholism, Substance Abuse and Addictions.

Miller, W.R., Meyers, R.J., & Tonigan, J.S. (1999). Engaging the unmotivated in treatment for alcohol problems: A comparison of three intervention strategies. *Journal of Consulting and Clinical Psychology.*

Minuchin, S., & Fishman, H.C. (1981). *Family therapy techniques.* Cambridge, MA: Harvard University Press.

Moos, R.H. (1990). Conceptual and empirical approaches to developing family-based assessment procedures: Resolving the case of the Family Environment Scale. *Family Process, 29,* 199-208.

Morrison. S.F., Rogers, P.D., & Thomas, M.H. (1995). Alcohol and adolescents. *Pediatric Clinics of North America, 42(2),* 371-387.

Nathan, P.E. (1990). Prevention and early intervention of addictive disorders. In H.B. Milkman & L.I. Sederer, (Eds.), *Treatment Choices for Alcoholism and Substance Abuse.* Lexington, MA: Lexington Books.

Newcomb, M.D., Huba, G.J., & Bentler, P.M. (1986). Life change events among adolescents: An empirical consideration of some methodological issues. *The Journal of Nervous and Mental Disease, 174(5),* 280-289.

Newcomb, M.D., Maddahian, E., Skagger, R., & Bentler, P.M. (1987). Substance abuse and psychosocial risk factors among teenagers: Associations with sex, age, ethnicity, and type of school. *American Journal of Drug and Alcohol Abuse, 13,* 413-433.

Paul, N.L. & Grosser, G. (1965). Operational mourning and its role in conjoint family therapy. *Community Mental Health Journal, 1,* 339-345.

Pickens, R.W., Leukefeld, C.G., & Schuster, C.R. (Eds.), (1991). *Improving Drug Abuse Treatment.* U.S. Department of Health and Human Services Pub. 91-1754. Rockville: National Institute on Drug Abuse.

Prochaska, J.O., di Clemente, C.C. & Norcross, J.C. (1992). In search of how people change: Applications to addictive behavior. *American Psychologist, 47,* 1102-1114.

Resnick, R.B., & Resnick, E.B. (1984). Cocaine abuse and its treatment. *Psychiatric Clinics of North America, 7(4),* 713-728.

Satir, V.M. (1981). *The new peoplemaking.* Palo Alto: Science and Behavior Books.

Seaburn, D., Landau-Stanton, J., Horwitz, S. (1995). Core techniques in family therapy. In R.H. Mikesell, D.D. Lusterman, & S.H. McDaniel (Eds.), *Integrating family therapy: Handbook of family psychology and systems theory* (pp. 5-26). Washington, D C: American Psychological Association Press.

Simpson, D.D., Joe, G.W., Rowan-Szal, G. & Greener, J. (1995). Client engagement and change during drug abuse treatment. *Journal of Substance Abuse, 7*, 117-134.

Speck, R.V., & Attneave, C. (1973). *Family networks*. New York: Pantheon.

Stanton, M.D. (1977). The addict as savior: Heroin, death in the family. *Family Process, 16(2):* 191-197.

Stanton, M.D. (1979). Family treatment approaches to drug abuse problems: A review. *Family Process, 18,* 251-280.

Stanton, M.D. (1981). An integrated structural/strategic approach to family therapy. *Journal of Marital and Family Therapy, 7*, 427-439.

Stanton, M.D. (1984). Breaking away: The use of strategic and Bowenian techniques in treating an alcoholic family through one member. In E. Kaufman (Ed.), *Power to change: Family case studies in the treatment of alcoholism* (pp. 253-266). New York: Gardner Press.

Stanton, M.D. (1992). The time line and the "why now?" question: A technique and rationale for therapy, training, organizational consultation and research. *Journal of Marital and Family Therapy, 18,* 331-343.

Stanton, M.D, & Heath, A. (1995). Family treatment of alcohol and drug abuse. In R.H. Mikesell, D.D. Lusterman, and S.H. McDaniel (Eds.), *Integrating family therapy: Handbook of family psychology and systems theory* (pp. 529-541). Washington, DC: American Psychological Association Press.

Stanton, M.D. & Heath, A. (1997). Family and marital therapy. In J.H. Lowinson, R.B. Millman, & J.G. Langrod (Eds.), *Substance abuse: A comprehensive textbook (3rd ed.*, pp. 448-454). Baltimore: Williams & Wilkins.

Stanton, M.D., & Landau, J. (1982). The family addiction cycle: A holistic family perspective. *Focus on Family and Chemical Dependency, 6(6).*

Stanton, M.D., & Landau, J. (1998). A model for alcoholism and addiction within the family: II. Intergenerational transmission, maintenance of the symptom, and therapeutic implications. Manuscript submitted for publication.

Stanton, M.D., Landau, J., Brinkman-Sull, D., Garrett, J., Shea, R., Baciewicz, G., & Browning, A. (1998). The ARISE approach to engaging reluctant alcohol- and drug-dependent individuals in treatment: Outcome and predictors. Manuscript submitted for publication.

Stanton, M. D., & Landau-Stanton, J. (1985). The family and substance abuse. In S. Henao and N. Grose (Eds.), *Principles of family systems in family medicine* (pp. 195-205). New York: Brunner/Mazel.

Stanton, M.D., & Landau-Stanton, J. (1990). Therapy with families of adolescent substance abusers. In H.B. Milkman, & L.I. Sederer (Eds.), *Treatment choices for alcoholism and substance abuse* (pp. 329-339). Lexington, MA: Lexington Books.

Stanton, M.D., & Shadish, W.R. (1997). Outcome, attrition, and family-couples treatment for drug abuse: A meta-analysis and review of the controlled, comparative studies. *Psychological Bulletin, 122(2),* 170-191.

Stanton, M.D., Todd, T.C., & Associates. (1982). *The family therapy of drug abuse and addiction.* New York: Guilford.

Stark, M.J. (1992). Dropping out of substance abuse treatment: A clinically oriented review. *Clinical Psychology Review, 12,* 93-116.

Startup, M., & Shapiro, D.A. (1993). Therapist treatment fidelity in prescriptive vs.

exploratory psychotherapy. *British Journal of Clinical Psychology, 32*, 443-456.

Suddaby, K., & Landau, J. (1998). Positive and negative timelines: A technique for restorying. *Family Process, 37(3),* 287-298.

Szapocznik, J., Perez-Vidal, A., Brickman, A.L., Foote, F.F., Santisteban, D., Hervis, O. & Kurtines, W.M. (1988). Engaging adolescent drug abusers and their families in treatment: A strategic structural systems approach. *Journal of Consulting and Clinical Psychology, 56(4)*, 552-557.

Thomas, E.J. & Ager, R.D. (1993). Unilateral family therapy with spouses of uncooperative alcohol abusers. In T.G. O'Farrell (Ed.). *Treating alcohol problems: Marital and family interventions.* New York: Guilford Press.

Whitaker, C.A., & Keith, D.V. (1981). Symbolic-experiential family therapy. In A. S. Gurman & D. S. Kniskern (Eds.), *Handbook of family therapy* (pp. 187-225). New York: Brunner/Mazel.

White, M. & Epston, D. (1990). *Narrative means to therapeutic ends.* New York: Norton.

Winters, K.C. & Zenilman, J. (1995). *Alcohol and other drug screening of hospitalized trauma patients.* Treatment Improvement Protocol (TIP) Series. U.S. Department of Health and Human Services, Substance Abuse and Mental Health Services Administration, Center for Substance Abuse Treatment.

ARISE & RESILIENCE PUBLICATIONS

Garrett, J. & Landau, J. (1998). ARISE: A Relational Intervention Sequence for Engagement—Training Manual for Supervisors and Trainers. Boulder, CO: Linking Human Systems, LLC.

Garrett, J. & Landau, J. (1999). ARISE: A Relational Intervention Sequence for Engagement—Training Manual for Certified ARISE Interventionists. Boulder, CO: Linking Human Systems, LLC.

Garrett, J. & Landau, J. (2001a). *Addiction Relapse Prevention During Traumatic Times: Part 1 -Questioning the 'Higher Power.'* Boulder: Holistic.com

Garrett, J. & Landau, J. (2001b). *Addiction Relapse Prevention During Traumatic Times: Part II - Resentments.* Boulder: Holistic.com

Garrett, J. & Landau, J. (2001c). *Addiction Relapse Prevention During Traumatic Times: Part III - Anger.* Boulder: Holistic.com

Garrett, J. & Landau, J. (2001d). *Addiction Relapse Prevention During Traumatic Times: Part IV - Fear,* Boulder: Holistic.com

Garrett, J. & Landau, J. (2001e). *Addiction Relapse Prevention During Traumatic Times: Part V - Sadness.* Boulder: Holistic.com

Garrett, J. & Landau, J. (In Press 2006a). Family Motivation to Change: A major factor in engaging alcoholics in treatment. By invitation for special issue of *Alcohol Treatment Quarterly.*

Garrett, J. & Landau, J. (In Press, 2006b). *Invitational Intervention: A Step-By-Step Guide for Getting Your Loved One into Addiction Treatment.* Binghamton, NY: Haworth Press.

Garrett, J. & Landau, J. (In Press, 2006c). *Invitational Intervention: A Step-By-Step Guide for Getting Your Loved One into Addiction Treatment.* www.BookSurgePublishing.com

Garrett, J., Landau, J., Stanton, M.D., Baciewicz, G., Brinkman-Sull, D., and Shea, R. (1998). The ARISE Intervention: Using family links to overcome resistance to addiction treatment. *Journal of Substance Abuse Treatment, 15(2),* 333-343.

Garrett, J., Landau-Stanton, J., Stanton, M. D., Baciewicz, G., Shea, R., & Brinkman Sull, D. (1996). ARISE: A manual for engaging substance abusers in treatment. University of Rochester (unpublished manual).

Garrett, J., Landau-Stanton, J., Stanton, M.D., Stellato-Kabat, J., & Stellato-Kabat, D. (1997). ARISE: A method for engaging reluctant alcohol- and drug-dependent individuals in treatment. *Journal of Substance Abuse Treatment, 13(5),* 1-14. Translated and republished in *Sistemas Familiares* (Argentina), 1998, *14(3),* 43-63. Translated and republished in (Hungary) (2001). ARISE - A kezelésre gyengén motivált drog- és alkoholfügg'k kezelésbe vonásának egyik módszere,. In G. Kelemen, B. Márta Erd's (Eds.), *Az addiktológia horizontja. Pécsi Orvostudományi Egyetem, Eü. F'iskolai Kar, Pécs,* 83--110.

Garrett, J., Stanton, M.D., Landau, J., Baciewicz, G., Brinkman-Sull, D., and Shea, R. (1999). The "Concerned Other" call: Using family links to overcome resistance to addiction treatment. *Substance Use and Misuse, 34(3),* 363-382.

Landau, J. (1997). Whispers of illness: Secrecy versus trust. In S.H. McDaniel, J. Hepworth, and W. Doherty (Eds.). *Stories in Medical Family Therapy.* New York: Basic Books.

Translated and republished in *Pensando Familias* (Brazil), 2005. *7(8)*, 9-20.

Landau, J. (2002). The Loss of Innocence: Personal Notes after September 11th, 2001. *Family Process, 41*, 27-30.

Landau, J. (2004). El modelo LINC: una estrategia colaborativa para la resiliencia comunitaria. *Sistemas Familiares, 20* (3); (English Translation available: The LINC Model: A Collaborative Strategy for Community Resilience.) Published in digital format at www.e-libro.com.

Landau, J., Cole, R., Tuttle, J., Clements, C.D. and Stanton, M.D. (2000). Family connectedness and women's sexual risk behaviors: Implications for the prevention/intervention of STD/HIV infection. *Family Process, 39(4)*, 461-475.

Landau, J. & Garrett, J. (In Press, 2006). *Invitational Intervention: A Step-by-Step Guide for Clinicians*. Binghamton, NY: Haworth Press.

Landau, J., Garrett, J., Shea, R., Stanton, M.D., Baciewicz, G., and Brinkman-Sull, D. (2000). Strength in Numbers: Using family links to overcome resistance to addiction treatment. *American Journal of Drug and Alcohol Abuse*, 26(3), 379-398.

Landau, J., Garrett, J., Shea, R., Stanton, M.D., Baciewicz, G., and Brinkman-Sull, D. (2002). A forca em números: O método ARISE para mobilizar familias e redes para engajar abusadores de substancia no tratamento. *Pensando Familias, 4 (4)*. 56-78.

Landau, J. & Hissett, J.L. (In press, 2007). Mild Traumatic Brain Injury: Impact on Identity and Ambiguous Loss in the Family. *Family Relations, 56(2)*.

Landau J. & Saul, J. (2004a). Facilitando a Resiliência da Familia e da Comunidade em Resposta a Grandes Desastres. *Pensando Familias, 6 (7)*. 35-66.

Landau, J., & Saul, J. (2004b). Facilitating family and community resilience in response to major disaster. In F. Walsh & M. McGoldrick (eds.), *Living Beyond Loss* (pp. 285-309). New York: Norton.

Landau, J., Stanton, M.D., Brinkman-Sull, D., Ikle, D., McCormick, D., Garrett, J., Baciewicz, G., Shea, R., Wamboldt, F. (2004). Outcomes with the ARISE approach to engaging reluctant drug- and alcohol-dependent individuals in treatment. *American Journal of Drug & Alcohol Abuse, 30(4)*.

Landau J., & Weaver, A. M. (In Press, 2006) The LINC Model of Community Resilience: Policy Implications for Disaster Preparedness, Response & Recovery. *Journal of Family & Consumer Sciences. Volume 98, Issue 2*.

Landau-Stanton, J. Competence, impermanence, and transitional mapping: A model for systems consultation. (1986). In L.C. Wynne, S. McDaniel, and T. Weber (eds.), *Systems Consultations -- A New Perspective for Family Therapy*. New York: Guilford Press, p. 253.
     Republication (In press) *Sistemas Familiares* (Argentina) and *South African Marital and Family Therapy Newsletter*.

Landau-Stanton, J. (1990). Issues and methods of treatment for families in cultural transition. In. M.P. Mirkin (Ed.), *The Social and Political Context of Family Therapy*. Needham Heights, Mass.: Allyn and Bacon.

Landau-Stanton, J., Clements, C., and Associates. (1993). *AIDS, Health and Mental Health: A Primary Sourcebook*. New York: Brunner/Mazel, Inc.

Loneck, B., Garrett, J.A., Banks, S.M. (1996a). A comparison of the Johnson Intervention with four other methods of referral to outpatient treatment. *American Journal of Drug and Alcohol Abuse, 22(2)*, 233-246.

Loneck, B., Garrett, J.A., Banks, S.M. (1996b). The Johnson Intervention and Relapse during outpatient treatment. *American Journal of Drug and Alcohol Abuse, 22(3)*, 363-375.

Seaburn, D., Landau–Stanton, J. and Horwitz, S. (1995). Core intervention techniques in family therapy process. In R.H. Mikesell, D.D. Lusterman, and S.H. McDaniel (Eds.), *Integrating Family Therapy: Handbook of Family Psychology and Systems Theory.* Washington, DC: American Psychological Association.

Stanton, M. D., Adams, E., Landau, J., & Black, G. S., (1997). Names as "scripts" in the family transmission of drug and alcohol abuse patterns: Results from a national survey. Unpublished manuscript, University of Rochester and the Gordon S. Black Corporation.

Suddaby, K., and Landau, J. (1998). Positive and negative timelines: A technique for restorying. *Family Process, 37(3)*, 287-298.
   Translated and republished in *Pensando Famílias,* (Brazil), 2002, *4(4)*, 56-78.

Tuttle, J.; Landau, J.; Stanton, M.D.; King, K.; Frodi , A. (2004). Intergenerational Family Relations and Sexual Risk Behavior in Young Women. *The American Journal of Maternal Child Nursing.*

Weine, S., Ukshini, S., Griffith, J., Agani, F., Pulleyblank-Coffey, E., Ulaj, J., Becker, C., Ajeti, L., Griffith, M., Alidemaj-Sereqi, V., Landau, J., Asllani, M., Pavkovic, I., Bunjaku, A., Rolland, J., Cala, G., Saul, J., Makolli, S., Sluzki, C., Statovci, S. (2005) A Family Approach to Severe Mental Illness in Post-War Kosovo. *Psychiatry, Spring 2005; 68*, 1: Academic Research Library pg. 17.

PREVIEW OF UPCOMING BOOK:

Invitational Intervention:
A Step-by-Step Guide for Getting Your Loved One into Treatment

JAMES GARRETT
AND DR. JUDITH LANDAU

DR. JUDITH LANDAU AND JAMES GARRETT

PREFACE

All too often, we hear that a person with an addiction problem must "hit bottom" and be self-motivated to get help before treatment will work. It is interesting to think of these beliefs in the context of the beginning of Alcoholics Anonymous. Did Ebby T. seek help on his own? Did Bill W. ask for help when he entered detox for the last time? Did Dr. Bob ask for help when his now celebrated meeting with Bill W. in Akron took place? Did Charles D., the third man to get sober using AA, seek help on his own? The answer to each of these questions is NO.

Ebby T. was approached by Rowland H., taken to his first Oxford Group meeting, and stopped drinking when he began to attend these meetings. He, in turn, approached an intoxicated Bill W. in his apartment and took him to Townes Hospital in New York City. Bill never drank again after that hospitalization. Bill W. sought out Dr. Bob—not the other way around. Finally, Bill W. and Dr. Bob asked the nurses if any of their patients were in the hospital due to alcohol related problems and then made an unsolicited visit to Charles D. in his hospital bed.

We would not have AA today were it not for the unsolicited and courageous "interventions" set in motion by these individuals instrumental in starting AA. It is in the AA tradition to reach out and help the "sick and suffering alcoholic." This tradition has been adopted and honored by the other 12 Step programs that have followed, for example—Narcotics Anonymous, Gamblers Anonymous, Sex and Love Addicts Anonymous, and Overeaters Anonymous. This tradition can best be seen in the following writing of Bill W., co-founder of AA. He writes about the early experience of having to change how the new comer into AA was approached, because the newer members were not as advanced in their addiction as the first members had been. These newer members were coming into AA because of outreach efforts and other "interventions" designed to get alcoholics the help they needed at an earlier point in the addiction. The results have been astounding, sparing individuals many years of suffering by getting them started in recovery, in-spite of their initial resistance or unwillingness.

"For years we old-timers simply could not communicate with such folks," meaning the newcomers who had not hit bottom. "Then, out of much experience, a new approach was developed. To each new high-bottom, we emphasized the medical view that alcoholism is a fatal and progressive malady." P249
"It is probable that one-half of today's AA membership has been spared that last five, ten, or even fifteen years of unmitigated hell that we low-bottoms know all too well." P294
Language of the Heart, Bill W's Grapevine Writings, 1988

The ARISE (A Relational Intervention Sequence for Engagement) method of Invitational Intervention is built on this same principal of reaching out to the "sick and suffering" individual. ARISE uses the concern, worry, sadness, frustration and anger of those affected by addiction to motivate the resistant AI to enter treatment and/or attend self-help meetings. Once an Intervention Network of family, friends, co-workers and concerned others is committed to meet, they invite the AI to attend the Intervention meetings right from the start. The openness, respect and love in this Invitational Intervention process results in a "win-win" outcome for both the Intervention Network members and the AI.

What surprises many people, including addiction treatment professionals, is that the authors' research from a National Institute of Drug Abuse (NIDA) grant (RO1 DA09402) shows that when the ARISE protocol is followed six out of ten AI's attend the first Intervention meeting. One of the keys to a successful ARISE Intervention is for the Intervention Network to agree to meet and to continue meeting, regardless of whether the AI attends any or all of the planned Intervention meetings. When families attend Intervention meetings, they demonstrate a commitment that we call Family Motivation to Change™. The research on the ARISE method shows that by the end of three-to-five Intervention meetings, eight out of ten AIs are in treatment or attending self-help meetings.

The ARISE method is very different from most of the other popular Intervention methods. It emphasizes the process of building motivation, as opposed to staging a one-time event that is designed to hammer through resistance. The ARISE method is a three-level Invitational Intervention, starting with Level I, "The First Call" by a "Concerned Other" (CO) member of the addicted person's support network, who wants help with getting a loved one started in treatment. The three levels are designed to respect the family's long-term investment and enhance their relationship commitment to their addicted loved one. Every family and every situation is different. Each Intervention Network is in charge of the direction and strategic plan that will best support their addicted love one's getting into treatment.

Level I sets up the first Intervention Network meeting. Level II ARISE Intervention Network meetings follow if the AI has not entered treatment or started attending self-help meetings during Level I. Only if Level II is not successful, is there a formal ARISE Intervention—Level III. The aim is to help get the addicted person into treatment with the least amount of effort or confrontation.

The ARISE method incorporates the most current understanding of addiction, the ability to work with the competence and strengths of the family, and state-of-the-art knowledge about the process of motivation to change. Parts II, III, and IV in this book correspond to Levels I, II, and III of the ARISE method. These three sections provide a practical, step-by-step guide for the reader. We hope you use them as a map, looking at them many times over, to help you get to your eventual destination. We suggest using a Certified ARISE Interventionist when doing an Invitational Intervention and not going it alone. We suggest this because of the long-term nature of the method and the commitment to continued meetings, regardless of whether or not the addicted individual enters treatment.

The book also offers a number of questionnaires and informational resources to help you both determine the severity of the problem you are dealing with and decide whether to start an ARISE intervention at this time. Our experience is that many families decide very quickly to contact an ARISE Interventionist, while other families take a little longer before taking action. Don't get discouraged if you and your Intervention Network group need to take a little more time before contacting an ARISE Interventionist. The very fact that you are considering doing something is the start of change! Remember, most addicted individuals enter treatment and eventually get into recovery because of "a nudge, a judge or with a grudge." The key ingredient is for someone to get the change process started. We hope that the ARISE method will help you be successful in getting a resistant loved one into recovery.

Throughout the book, you will find brief vignettes to illustrate some of the ARISE methods, and to help you identify with the many common situations that families confront when living with an active addiction. All identifying information about these individuals and their families has been removed to protect their confidentiality. Some of the examples are composite families, designed to give you a taste of what you might experience, should you choose to do an ARISE Invitational Intervention and get your loved one into treatment.

CHAPTER 1
Is There A Stranger In Your Home?

Approach each new problem not with a view of finding what you hope will be there, but to get the truth, the realities that must be grappled with. You may not like what you find. In that case, you are entitled to try to change it.
Bernard M. Baruch

Very often we hear a family member, or Concerned Other (CO), of an addicted person's support network say, "I don't even know who this person is any more. S/he has changed so much s/he has become a total stranger. If only there was a way to get him/her back." How is it that a loved one can change right in front of us and leave us feeling hopeless and helpless to stop the self-destruction? How is it that a problem as obvious as addiction can be so hard to spot? How is it that instinctive responses by family members to an addiction can often make the problem worse, when the clear intention is to get the loved one back functioning in a healthy way? How does the Addicted Individual (AI) become so powerful that relationships, communications, and problem solving become a one-on-one series of battles with the addiction winning time after time?

This chapter is designed to help answer these questions and to give you, the reader, an opportunity to take action to get your loved one back through a loving and carefully planned process we call ARISE—A Relational Intervention Sequence for Engagement. First, we will help you decide whether you are living with, and have been seriously affected by, an addiction problem. Second, we will help you understand how your loved one became a stranger right in front of your eyes. And third, we will help you decide whether or not, as Vanzant states, you are "Ready to declare **W-A-R!** I declare: I am now **W**illing, **A**ble and **R**eady to stop addiction in its tracks and reclaim my family and my future." P133.

Let's begin to look at whether you have been seriously impacted by living with an addiction problem. This may not be as obvious as it might seem. The reason for this is that people living with addiction begin to adapt their feelings, thoughts, and behaviors in response to the addiction. The adaptations are made in an attempt to maintain some sense of balance and normal functioning in the face of the problem.

Unfortunately, the adaptations become increasingly dysfunctional as the addiction progresses down a destructive path. Family and close friends begin to isolate, feel an over-whelming sense of shame, guilt, worry, sadness, confusion, frustration, and anger in response to the deceit, lying, irrational thinking, and denial from the Addicted Individual. The following family description will help clarify this notion of adaptation. If you can identify with a number of the situations in this case example, you may want to explore further the options of doing an Invitational Intervention. This family example is a composite of the many families we have helped with the ARISE method.

We would like to introduce the Vann family. Their genogram—or family tree—is drawn below. Carl is a middle manager for an insurance company. He is 42 and has been married to Irene, age 40, for 16 years. Irene is a registered nurse who works three-day weekend shifts at the local hospital. Both Carl and Irene are African-American, involved with their Baptist Church, and have three children.

Sam is 17 years old and a senior in high school. He excels in sports, has below-average grades, and intends move into an apartment with friends after high school and attend the local community college. Jane is 14 and a freshman in high school. She is a straight-A student and participates in many clubs at school. Ben, the youngest, just turned six. He is in kindergarten and there is concern that he may have Attention Deficit Disorder (ADD) as he has begun to exhibit some acting-out behavior.

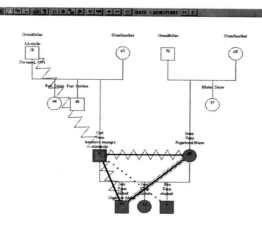

Carl's father was an abusive alcoholic. Carl vowed as an adolescent that he would never drink like his father. He typically drinks on weekends and especially enjoys Sunday afternoons watching sports on TV and drinking with his buddies. This means he often comes home early Sunday evening after an afternoon of drinking. Sometimes when he gets home, the slightest things can easily annoy him. The children may be too noisy, he may want to roughhouse at the time the children are quieting down, or he may pick a fight with Irene over financial problems. From the time their first child was born, Irene developed a pattern of feeding them early, having a meal on the table for Carl when he got home, and having the children in bed as early as possible. She did these things in order to minimize conflict and protect the children from exposure to their arguments before going to bed.

On the surface, Irene's behavior is completely understandable. She might even be praised for protecting her children. However, over time and as the children get older, things at home began to change. The children started to question why they couldn't watch a favorite TV program on a Sunday evening, and why their father acts so differently when he comes home Sunday evenings. Sam starts to have school problems and drops off the football team, Jane spends more and more time alone in her bedroom reading and listening to music, and Ben is already behind in his reading ability, and has trouble concentrating and listening to directions.

After years of living with her husband's drinking, Irene starts to feel overwhelmed, isolated, and very angry with both her husband and the children. The household is filled with stress most of the time and the family spends less and less healthy, loving time together. After some ten years of marriage, Carl begins to drink after work on some weekdays, something he has not done before. Irene begins to question herself, because Carl tells her that she has nothing to worry about. He says he doesn't drink that much, doesn't need it, and in fact, is now drinking after work because of the increasing pressure he has from his job. He pays less and less attention to Irene and shows little affection to her. Their marriage and family are no longer what they were, nor what they hoped for. He has become a stranger to her.

As Irene becomes more and more stressed, and filled with self-doubt, anger, and worry, she begins to change many of her own behaviors. (These stress-induced symptoms and behaviors are outlined in the following table, Effects of Living With Addiction: Self-Questionnaire, figure 1.1). Irene may not even know that she is experiencing these stress-induced symptoms as a result of living with her husband's increasingly serious drinking problem over the past eight to ten years. There is a gradual, but steady progression in her symptoms, including increasing self-doubt, outbursts of anger, frequent headaches and stomach pains, isolation from her family and friends, and having an affair with someone from the hospital.

The children are also acting out more and more, frequently challenging their parents' authority. Carl's drinking escalates. All of these symptoms develop simultaneously, making it difficult to determine the origin of the problem that started them in the first place. Are her anxious feelings and loss of appetite a result of the financial stresses and her affair? Are the marital problems because of her lack of sexual desire and her husband's complaints about not having enough sex in their marriage? Or, does the children's fighting cause her stomach pains and headaches?

Where and how did Carl's drinking get lost in the evolution of the family and in the increasing stress on his wife to keep the family together? Carl has gradually changed and evolved into the man, his father that he had vowed not to be like. His children are growing up in a home similar to the one in which he was raised. In fact, after witnessing a particularly loud recent argument between his parents, Sam said to himself, "I'll never treat my wife like that," even though for the past year he has been smoking marijuana on a regular basis.

In spite of the best intentions, the Vann family has become an "alcoholic family." Carl is thinking and behaving in black and white—all or nothing terms, with threats of separation, arguments in front of the children, and frequent episodes of screaming at both Irene and the children. Irene is angry, mistrustful, controlling, and resentful much of the time, and feels like a Victim—helpless and trapped. Sam is becoming the "Acting Out" or "Scapegoat Child," filled with his own anger and fears. Jane is acting the "Hero Child," trying to be perfect in hopes of ending the family's stress, and Ben has become the "Lost Child," feeling alone and scared most of the time. Each of them is suffering deeply, yet none of them has any idea how to change the situation.

This scenario can develop for pretty much any relationship dynamic, whether it is among siblings, parents, and children or between work colleagues or good friends. The particulars might vary—i.e., compulsive gambling, drug addiction, Internet addiction, eating disorder—and the individual symptoms might be different; but the outcome is almost always the same. The addicted person is engaged primarily in a one-on-one battle denying the problem. One-on-one the addiction *always* wins. This vignette demonstrates how addiction develops, progresses, and ultimately goes untreated. The individuals living with the addiction become a part of the problem and increasingly are less able to initiate meaningful change.

Are you concerned that someone you care about, or live with, may be developing problems caused by an addiction? For example, drinking too heavily, using drugs, gambling, spending too much, having sequential sexual affairs, compulsively shopping, or spending a great deal of time on the Internet? If your answer is, "Yes," we offer you a set of questions that will help to determine whether you are being seriously impacted by "living with" an addiction.

Regardless of the type of addiction—drugs, alcohol, compulsive gambling, sexual acting out, eating, or Internet—the symptoms of those affected follow a predictable course. We have developed the Effects of Living With Addiction: Self-Questionnaire (see Figure 1.1), to help you step back from the "heat of the battle" and take a more objective look at yourself and the situation. We suggest doing an exercise. First, familiarize yourself with the questionnaire. Then follow the exercise outlined in the next few paragraphs. As hard as it may be, be honest with yourself.

The Effects of Living With Addiction: Self-Questionnaire is divided into three columns. The first column is labeled "Mental and Emotional State." The series of descriptive words in this column is taken from the body of research related to the impact of addiction on those who live with it. The five categories are: anger, fear/worry, controlling/nagging, avoiding, and denial. They are the most common feelings and mental reactions that develop from living with an addiction problem over an extended period. Start by looking at your past week. Ask yourself if you can identify strongly with any one or a combination of these five states. Write down the situations that occurred in your past week that seem to correspond with each state to which you relate. For example, you might write down the word "nagging." When you think back on the last week, you might remember feeling this "nagging" reaction to situations where you became bossy and demanding because you did not feel listened to.

The second column is labeled "Behaviors." The typical behaviors listed correspond to each "Mental and Emotional State." On the same sheet of paper, write down any relevant behaviors of yours from the past week. Are you beginning to identify a pattern of feeling and behavior?

The third column is labeled "Identification Questions." Now, go down the list, ask yourself whether or not in the past week you have experienced any of them and answer, "yes" if you have. Then, as you look at what you have written, ask yourself if there is a pattern to your thoughts, feelings, and behaviors. Ask yourself when these began to develop and whether they have become intrusive in your life. Ask yourself if any of these thoughts, feelings, and behaviors are related to the addictive behavior of a loved one. Ask yourself if you felt particular discomfort from this exercise. Ask yourself if you learned anything from the exercise.

Typically, the more "Identification Questions" you related to, the more likely it is that you are being strongly affected from living with an Addicted Individual. Use this exercise to help you gather information. You will go back to it later in the book when you ask yourself if *now* is the time to contact an ARISE Invitational Interventionist. Use this as a time for gathering information. If you feel comfortable, ask other family or friends to also do the exercise. Doing this exercise with a number of other individuals often opens up areas of discussion that are surprising, breaks the sense of isolation, and begins to build support when you realize that "no, you are not alone" and you no longer have to deal with the Addicted Individual one-on-one anymore.

Effects of Living With Addiction: Self Questionnaire		
Mental/Emotional State	Behavior	Identification Question
Anger	1. Getting into screaming matches 2. Being short tempered 3. Having aggressive outbursts 4. Becoming violent 5. Throwing things 6. Picking fights	1. Do I feel like I am beginning to lose it? 2. Is my anger turning to rage? 3. Do I have angry outbursts with people who don't deserve it? 4. Is my tendency to become violent scaring me? 5. Am I involved in risk taking behavior, e.g., driving carelessly, getting involved in an affair, or tempted to gamble?
Fear/Worry	1. "Walking on egg shells" 2. Being on edge 3. Sensing something bad is going to happen 4. Blaming yourself for the behavior of others	1. Am I having trouble sleeping? 2. Am I having frequent headaches? 3. Is my stomach frequently in knots? 4. Am I starting to over-spend or over-eat? 5. Do I wake up with my pulse racing and a feeling of dread?
Controlling/Nagging	1. Making threats 2. Becoming more and more controlling 3. Not wanting to let the person out of your sight 4. Frequently complaining about the other person's behavior 5. Feeling that you are always right	1. Am I nervous most of the time? 2. Do I have trouble relaxing? 3. Am I more critical of others than I used to be? 4. Am I tired a lot? 5. Am I feeling lonely? 6. Do my thoughts shift from preoccupation with the problem to completely wanting to give up?
Avoiding	1. Becoming more and more isolated from family and friends 2. Not going out 3. Feeling more and more uncomfortable in social situations 4. Not wanting to go to work	1. Do I doubt myself? 2. Am I fearful of what others are thinking of my family situation and me? 3. Am I spending a lot of time alone? On the Internet? 4. Am I developing anxiety symptoms? 5. Has someone suggested I may be depressed? 6. Am I starting to drink more than usual, take sleeping pills or medication for anxiety?
Denial	1. Not believing that an addiction might be the problem 2. Lying to others about situations that occurred 3. Becoming more and more guilty	1. Do I find myself covering up the truth when I know it is a lie? 2. Have I begun to have vague physical symptoms that cannot be medically diagnosed? 3. Am I often sad and sometimes find that I cry myself to sleep?

So now that you have discovered whether you are being affected by living with an addiction, the next question to ask yourself is, "How did this happen?" "How did this person I know so well become a stranger?" The short answer to this question lies in the functioning of the brain. Recent scientific advances show that a dynamic series of changes to the brain structure, brain neuro-chemistry and brain function occurs as the result of a long-standing addiction. Every substance has what is termed a "capture rate." This capture rate is a measure of the potential of a particular substance to become addictive.

In other words, if someone uses this particular substance, how strong is the likelihood of that person becoming addicted to it. The combination of the "capture rate" and such factors as genetic predisposition, death of a loved one, trauma, and multiple life stresses result in an individual being vulnerable to addiction. The individual initially takes a substance to "party" and feel good. Along the way, for AIs, the good times from getting high turn to using the substance as a way to avoid dealing with life issues, feelings, growing up and other stressors.

The same principal applies to other addictive behaviors that do not involve putting a substance into the body, i.e., gambling, sex, food, shopping and Internet. What often starts out as seeking fun and relaxing, eventually turns on the individual and becomes the source of the problems. Addiction is best understood by three characteristics: 1) a loss of control; 2) continued use in-spite of adverse consequences; and 3) denial, rationalization and minimization of the problem behavior in-spite of the negative consequences. Let's look at what each of these items mean:

1) Loss of control means that a person is not able to predict what will happen to him/her on a consistent basis once s/he starts to use the drug. The best example of this is with an alcoholic who at times can limit the drinking to one or two drinks, and at other times finds that one or two lead to intoxication and negative consequences. Social drinkers do not experience loss of control.

2) Continued use, in-spite of negative consequences, is marked by the individual's continuing the specific behavior (alcohol/drug use, gambling, sexual acting out, compulsive spending, or compulsive eating) that others objectively see as a problem, regardless of the problems that result from it.

An example of this is when an individual addicted to pain medication sees two or three different physicians in order to get multiple prescriptions, regardless of the medical danger from this over use.

3) Denial, rationalization, and minimization of the problem behavior are the result of the development of new defense mechanisms designed to prevent the individual from seeing and acknowledging the truth about the hurt and pain that the problem behavior is causing. An example of denial, rationalization, and minimization is when a person becomes secretive about sexual acting-out and justifies the behavior by convincing him/herself that "everyone acts this way," or "I am just going through a phase. I'll stop this when it gets to be a problem," or "Guys are just different. What she doesn't know won't hurt her."

The AI is not able to see the reality of the problem behavior because of changes to his/her brain structure and brain function. S/he has lost the ability to control the problem behavior because the messages coming from the brain are no longer rational and sequential. It gets to the point where s/he deliberately continues the behavior to try to get control of him/herself and to convince others that there is no addiction problem. That is why it is so often said, "that the first drink gets you drunk."

The first drink, drug use, gambling wager, etc., starts a complex chain reaction in the brain that eventually results in the individual wanting more and more. The addicted brain kicks in and makes all of the decisions from the unconscious viewpoint of "if a little makes me feel good, more will make me feel better." Once addicted, the individual is not capable of using the rational part of the brain (cortex), and is left with decisions coming from a deep brain center known as the "Reptilian brain" that operates completely on getting immediate gratification and pleasure.

The AI has lost the ability to see the seriousness of the addiction, and denies the problem behavior because the main part of the brain now working is functioning to maintain the addiction. Anyone or anything that threatens continuation of the behavior is seen in the most negative way because once the brain changes to addictive thinking the most important function is to protect the addictive behavior.

The addictive behavior develops as a result of continued loss of control, continued use in-spite of consequences, and the formation of denial, rationalization, and minimization. Addictive thinking has the sole purpose of protecting the individual from acknowledging the root and seriousness of the problem. The addict is the only one who does not believe there is a problem.

These brain changes occur regardless of the drug used or the compulsive behavior that is exhibited. The only variant is that different drugs and different behaviors affect different neural pathways. For instance, alcohol, marijuana, and nicotine all activate the same addictive neural pathway in the limbic part of the brain. Cocaine and meth activate a different neural pathway by flooding the brain with dopamine—a powerful, but short acting stimulant.

Recent research using Magnetic Resonance Imaging (MRI) technology shows similar brain changes in the dopamine pathways in sexual addicts and compulsive gamblers. Please take a look at the bibliography at the end of Section I for scientific references and additional readings about the brain changes that result in addiction. We believe that the scientific research validates our understanding that addiction is a disease. Literally, the brain is malfunctioning. *The only way* to correct the problem is to stop the behavior that activates the addicted part of the brain.

We hope that understanding these brain changes helps you to know how you have "come to live with a stranger." Truly, the person you now are interacting with is not the same person you used to know. The sad reality is that most AIs never get into treatment and never recover from the addiction, because they are not able to see the reality of the problem. The world is seen through "addicted eyes." In most situations, it takes others to point out the seriousness of the addiction and to put a degree of pressure on them in order to effect change. Rarely is the Addicted Individual able to do this on his/her own. We believe that loved ones and concerned others are in a powerful position to help in this change process. The ARISE method is meant to guide loved ones and concerned others to help the addicted person get into treatment and start a recovery journey.

APPENDIX A

FORMS, CONTRACTS, CHECKLISTS, SCREENING TOOLS & ONLINE ASSESSMENTS

DR. JUDITH LANDAU AND JAMES GARRETT

SAMPLE ARISE INTERVENTION AGREEMENT

ARISE Intervention Services and Payment Agreement
There are two ways to pay for the ARISE Intervention service.

The first is by paying for each session as it occurs, the second is to enter into a flat fee agreement. In either event, the services cover the same ground and continue until the individual has been in recovery for a period of 6 months. If you choose to continue further than 6 months of recovery, we charge by the hour.

1. Agreement to work with the Recovery Resource Center to do an ARISE Intervention: Individual Session Payment.
We agree to work with each other to do an ARISE Intervention. The following are the terms of the agreement.

1. The Cost of the Individual Session Payment for the ARISE Intervention:
The recommended cost for the ARISE Intervention services is $90-350/hour (dependent on level of experience of ARISE Interventionist) per hour for ARISE Interventionists with a sliding fee scale available upon request. We do not bill insurance for these services because they are not considered as treatment and insurance will only cover treatment. Travel costs, when required, are billed separately and in addition. Much of the ARISE Intervention service can be provided on the telephone or via email.
2. The Intervention work is divided into two phases.
a. The first phase includes the preparatory work for the Intervention, the ARISE Intervention network session(s) and necessary follow-up sessions to facilitate entry into treatment.
b. The second phase services involve: advising, screening and selection recommendations for inpatient and/or outpatient treatment; interface between the Intervention network and

the treatment provider; coordination of aftercare; integration planning if the individual is returning home or to the community; advice on using self-help meetings, and setting up a self help support network; addressing questions related to ongoing treatment and other functioning related issues; relapse prevention; and emergency meetings if relapse occurs. These functions are Recovery Management Services, essential in the first 6 months of recovery. Typically, these services in the second phase extend over a 6—month period following the individual's beginning treatment, because it is important to build in monitoring and accountability to ensure lasting recovery.

c. If you choose to continue using Recovery Management Services beyond the 6-month period, sessions are charged at an individual session rate of $90-350/hour (dependent on level of experience of ARISE Interventionist) per hour. Payment is due after each session.

OR

2. Agreement to work with the Recovery Resource Center to do an ARISE Intervention: Flat Fee Agreement

1. The Recovery Resource Center only commits to offering an ARISE Intervention when the Concerned Other member (CO) of the support system who contacts the Center agrees to participate in both phases 1 and 2. The recommended cost for the first phase is $3-10,000 (dependent on level of experience of ARISE Interventionist) per ARISE Interventionist. Payment is due at the time the ARISE sessions start. In cases of serious recidivism, the services of 2 Senior ARISE Interventionists may be required.

3. The recommended cost for the second phase is $3-10,000 (dependent on level of experience of ARISE Interventionist), payable when, and only if, the individual about whom the CO has contacted the Recovery Resource Center enters treatment. Treatment is defined as starting any level of outpatient or inpatient care, or beginning to attend self-help meetings.

a. The first phase includes the preparatory work for the Intervention, the ARISE Intervention network session(s) and the necessary follow-up sessions to facilitate entry into treatment.

b. The second phase services involve: the advising, screening and selection recommendations for inpatient and/or outpatient treatment; interface between the Intervention network and the treatment provider; coordination of aftercare; integration planning if the individual is returning home or to the community; advice on beginning to use self help meetings, and setting up a self help support network; addressing questions related to ongoing treatment and other functioning related issues; relapse prevention; and emergency meetings if relapse occurs. These functions are Recovery Management Services, essential in the first 6 months of recovery. Typically, these services in the second phase extend over a 6—month period following the individual's beginning treatment, because it is important to build in monitoring and accountability to ensure lasting recovery.

c. If you choose to continue using Recovery Management Services beyond the 6-month period, sessions are charged at an individual session rate of $90-350/hour (dependent on level of experience of ARISE Interventionist).

(CONCERNED OTHER COPY)

I acknowledge by my signature below that I have read and carefully reviewed and am familiar with the contents of the information enclosed and agree to the conditions described in the contract. If I have any questions or would like additional information, I will feel free to ask.

_____   _____   _____
Concerned Other (print)   Date   Signature

_____   _____   _____
Concerned Other (print)   Date   Signature

_____   _____   _____
Concerned Other (print)   Date   Signature

_____   _____   _____
Interventionist (print)   Date   Signature

INTERVENTION AGREEMENT

(ARISE INTERVENTIONIST COPY)

I acknowledge by my signature below that I have read and carefully reviewed and am familiar with the contents of the information enclosed and agree to the conditions described in the contract. If I have any questions or would like additional information, I will feel free to ask.

_____   _____   _____
Concerned Other (print)   Date   Signature

_____   _____   _____
Concerned Other (print)   Date   Signature

_____   _____   _____
Concerned Other (print)   Date   Signature

_____   _____   _____
Interventionist (print)   Date   Signature

ARISE FIRST CALL WORKSHEET

Caller's name:_____ Date:_____

Caller's phone #:_____ email:_____

Address:_____ Relationship to AI:_____

1. Presenting Problem (Join, Address Caller's Initial Concerns, Identify Presenting Problem)

2. Get Permission to Ask More Personal Questions

3. Construct a Preliminary Genogram (use back of this page or separate page)

4. Construct list of support network members to invite to 1st meeting

5. Get Substance Abuse History

6. Get Brief Treatment History (include self help, use of sponsor and any form of treatment received)

7. Identify Past Family Efforts (join around AI manipulation and breaking one-on-one isolation)

8. Assess for Safety
    a. Is the AI threatening to hurt him/herself or anyone else? (Are there weapons involved?)
    b. Has someone needed to call the police recently? (Explore details)
    c. Has the AI been involved in any serious accidents lately? (Explore details)
    d. Has there been any history of domestic violence or abuse?

9. Finalize who to invite to form the Intervention Network and get commitment to attend regardless of whether or not the addicted individual attends

10. Finalize time and place to hold the First Meeting

11. Develop Recovery Message and strategy to invite the Addicted Individual

INVITATIONAL INTERVENTION

SAMPLE ARISE INTERVENTION NETWORK AGREEMENT

ADDICTED INDIVIDUAL'S AGREEMENT	INTERVENTION NETWORK AGREEMENT
1. I agree to abstain from using any drugs or alcohol.	1. I agree to remove all drugs and alcohol from the home for a minimum of six months.
2. If I do use any drugs or alcohol, I agree to start inpatient treatment immediately.	2. If my loved one uses any drugs or alcohol, I agree to enforce and assist him/her in starting inpatient treatment immediately.
3. I will attend meetings with the ARISE Interventionist and the Intervention Network.	3. I will attend meetings with the ARISE Interventionist, my loved one and the Intervention Network.
4. I will expect/accept natural consequences of my behavior and not expect the family to intervene on my behalf: e.g., detention, suspension from school, removal from basketball team, police intervention and jail.	4. I will allow natural consequences to take place, regardless of their severity and my loved one's pleas.
5. I will contact _____ and/or _____ if I need support, if I feel the need to, or do use any drugs or alcohol.	5. I will be available to my loved one for support.

SAMPLE ARISE INTERVENTION NETWORK AGREEMENT

(Continued)

In case of an emergency, I will call:

_____   or   _____

I have read and understand the obligations and responsibilities. In addition, I make a personal commitment to follow the agreed upon recovery goals.

Client signature: _____   Date:_____

    Intervention Network Signatures:

    Date:_____   _____
                              Relationship to Client

    Date:_____   _____
                              Relationship to Client

    Witness:_____   _____
                              Relationship to Client

    Date:_____   _____
                              ARISE Interventionist

SOBER SUPPORT
INTERVENTION NETWORK AGREEMENT

CHEMICALLY DEPENDENT PERSON'S AGREEMENT	SOBER SUPPORT NETWORK AGREEMENT
1. I agree to abstain from all mood-altering substances, including the cancellation of addictive prescription medication.	1. I agree to remove all mood-altering substances from the home for a minimum of six months.
2. I will agree to B.A.C. or urine testing requested by my therapist and/or support network.	2. I will be available to the client for support of the treatment plan throughout withdrawal and early recovery.
3. I will participate with the treatment providers and the Sober Support Intervention Network to develop realistic early recovery goals.	3. I will collaborate with the client and the treatment providers to develop realistic early recovery goals.
4. I will expect/accept consequences of my behavior.	4. I will allow natural consequences to take place.
5. I will contact _____ and/or _____ if I relapse and will attend an emergency Sober Support Intervention Network session.	5. I will call/attend an emergency network session if there is a relapse by contacting the outpatient provider.

(Continued)

SOBER SUPPORT INTERVENTION NETWORK AGREEMENT

In case of an emergency, I will call:

_____ or _____

I have read and understand the obligations and responsibilities. In addition, I make a personal commitment to follow the agreed upon recovery goals.

Client signature: _____ Date: _____

Intervention Network Signatures:

Date: _____ _____

Relationship to Client

Date: _____ _____

Relationship to Client

Witness: _____ _____

Relationship to Client

Date: _____ _____

ARISE Interventionist

INVITATIONAL INTERVENTION

UNCOPE QUESTIONS TO SCREEN YOURSELF
FOR AN ALCOHOL OR DRUG ABUSE PROBLEM

The UNCOPE screening test consists of six questions found in existing instruments and assorted research reports. This excellent screening test was first reported by Hoffmann and colleagues in 1999. The six questions provide a simple and quick means of identifying whether you are at risk for abuse or dependence for alcohol and other drugs. Take the screening test and circle a "yes" or "no" at the end of each question. Answer the questions to the best of your knowledge—it may be difficult to be completely honest because of fears you might have about the outcome of this screening. You may find it interesting, informative and necessary to have others in your support network take the other screening test on this web site, "Alcohol and Drug Abuse---Assess Others." If you decide to compare your answers with theirs, you will likely have an interesting discussion. Your observations of your own behaviors over the past year may be quite different from others who also witnessed your drinking and drug use behaviors. The scoring of the screening test is found at the end of the six questions. Take the risk and stay as honest as possible when you answer the questions.

<u>U</u>   "In the past year, have you ever drank or **used** drugs more than you meant to?" Or "Have you spent more time drinking or **using** than you intended to?"

                    Yes   No

<u>N</u>   "Have you ever **neglected** some of your usual responsibilities because of using alcohol or drugs?"

                    Yes   No

C   "Have you wanted or needed to **cut down** on your drinking or drug use in the last year?"

          Yes   No

O   "Has anyone **objected** to your drinking or drug use?" or "Has your family, a friend, or anyone else ever told you they **objected** to your alcohol or drug use?"

          Yes   No

P   "Have you ever found yourself **preoccupied** with wanting to use alcohol or drugs?" or "Have you found yourself thinking a lot about drinking or using?"

          Yes   No

E   "Have you ever used alcohol or drugs to relieve **emotional discomfort**, such as sadness, anger, or boredom?"

          Yes   No

Two positive responses indicate a strong likelihood of an alcohol and/or drug abuse problem.

Four or more positive responses strongly indicate an alcohol and/or drug dependence problem.

UNCOPE QUESTIONS TO FAMILY AND CONCERNED OTHERS
TO SCREEN FOR AN ALCOHOL OR DRUG ABUSE PROBLEM

The UNCOPE screening test consists of six questions found in existing instruments and assorted research reports. This excellent screening test was first reported by Hoffmann and colleagues in 1999. The six questions provide a simple and quick means of identifying whether the person you are concerned about is at risk for abuse or dependence for alcohol and other drugs. Take the screening test and circle a "yes" or "no" at the end of each of the questions. Answer the questions to the best of your knowledge. You may find it interesting, comforting and necessary to have others in your support network take this screening test as well. It almost always will result in interesting discussion among those who take it because each person may have observed different drinking and drug use behaviors over the past year. The scoring of the screening test is found at the end of the six questions.

###

U "In the past year, have you ever observed the individual you are concerned about drinking or **using** drugs more than he/she meant to?"

Or "Have you noticed the person you are concerned about spending more time drinking or **using** than he/she intended to?"

                        Yes   No

N "Have you ever seen the individual you are concerned about **neglecting** some of his/her usual responsibilities because of using alcohol or drugs?"

                        Yes   No

C "Have you seen the individual you are concerned about wanting or needing to **cut down** on his/her drinking or drug use in the last year?"

                        Yes   No

O   "Have you or anyone else **objected** to the drinking or drug use of the individual you are concerned about?"

        Yes   No

P   "Have you ever found the individual you are concerned about **preoccupied** with wanting to use alcohol or drugs?"

Or, "Have you found the individual you are concerned about thinking and talking a lot about drinking or using?"

        Yes   No

E   "Have you ever observed or been worried that the individual you are concerned about is using alcohol or drugs to relieve **emotional discomfort**, such as sadness, anger, or boredom?"

        Yes   No

Two positive responses indicate a strong likelihood of an alcohol and/or drug abuse problem.

Four or more positive responses strongly indicate an alcohol and/or drug dependence problem.

APPENDIX B

WEB AND OTHER RESOURCES

DR. JUDITH LANDAU AND JAMES GARRETT

RESOURCES

Linking Human Systems, LLC: www.LinkingHumanSystems.com and

The Recovery Resource Center: www.RecoveryResourceCenter.com

Information available on these sites includes details for families regarding the ARISE Intervention, drugs, and simple evaluations for both the individual and Concerned Others to access alcohol/drug use.

The Following are Sample Excerpts from the Websites Listed Above:

Getting Started

I. How You Can Make a Difference in Getting a Loved One Started in Recovery

There are many examples of how families positively motivate and influence individuals to make productive and lasting changes. Think about what President Bush has publicly stated about his decision to stop drinking more than ten years ago. He stated that he quit drinking after his wife gave him an ultimatum, indicating that he could either keep drinking and face losing his marriage and family or he could stop drinking and have their love and support. He chose the latter.

Former First Lady Betty Ford was also faced with a similar decision relating to her drinking and prescription drug abuse. Her family met with her to discuss their worry and concerns about both the drinking and the prescription drug abuse. Again, she was faced with a difficult choice to stop using and get the needed love and support from her family for a lasting recovery or face the consequences of continued use. She chose to stop using and start recovery.

While these are two high-profile examples of how families can positively influence a loved one to stop using, numerous examples of "common folk" having success with the same technique are also common.

Please go to the Testimonials section in this web site for some case examples.

The key ingredient in each story is that the family became motivated to change. No longer was the family going to be controlled by the disease of addiction. No longer was the family going to "walk on egg shells" and be controlled by the guilt and blame used by the substance abuser. The family hits its own "bottom" and gets "sick and tired of being sick and tired". It takes only one in the family to start meaningful change. One person is capable of mobilizing others to join in stopping the destructive impact of untreated addiction on the family.

When this process of change starts, we call it Family Motivation to Change. If you are reading this, you are already in some stage of change. Focusing your energies by mobilizing others for support is the next step. We can help you get the addicted individual you are worried about started in treatment. Whether you are a parent concerned about an adult or adolescent child, a husband or wife concerned about a partner, a son/daughter concerned about a parent, a sibling concerned about a brother or sister, or a concerned other for a close friend or colleague, we can help you get the addicted individual started in treatment.

The ARISE method builds on the strengths and commitment of the Family Motivation to Change. The method matches the efforts used by the family to the resistance of the substance abuser. Our research shows that most substance abusers are willing to participate in a family meeting centered around the topic of their use when a loving and direct approach is used to invite them. We are trained to coach you in how best to approach your loved one. We know that you have a long-standing investment in your loved one's well-being and don't want to do anything to jeopardize that relationship. Addiction, on the other hand, can often tear a family apart if it goes untreated. As Certified ARISE Interventionists, we provide guidance and support for you in getting your loved one started in recovery.

II. The Courage to Talk with a Loved One Who Has a Drinking Problem

When an alcoholic seeks treatment, a family member, friend or a professional is typically the driving force behind the decision. Most alcoholics are reluctant to face their drinking problem. Remember, most alcoholics start treatment with a nudge, from the order of a Judge or with a grudge. Their reluctance to start treatment or lack of initial motivation has no bearing on the eventual outcome. It may be up to you to break through the denial and start the recovery process for someone you know. It will not be easy to intervene constructively, but it can save the life of your friend or relative. The ARISE Intervention is a respectful method of breaking through the denial system.

"In most cases, a spouse or close relative knows enough about a person's drinking pattern to recognize when it is a serious problem and possibly alcoholism," says Robert M. Morse, M.D., a Mayo Clinic psychiatrist who specializes in the diagnosis and treatment of alcoholism. Alcoholics and alcohol abusers are not the only ones who may use denial. Their family members or friends may use denial as a coping mechanism, too. Over time, denial is destructive for all involved.

The National Institute on Alcohol Abuse and Alcoholism estimates that 14 million Americans—one of every 13 adults—either abuse alcohol or are alcoholics. Dr. Morse says alcoholism is "horribly under-diagnosed." The risk of developing alcoholism is present at any age. Teen-agers may be especially vulnerable, but you can become an alcoholic much later in life as well.

Alcoholism
Alcoholism is an addiction to alcohol. It is often progressive and can be fatal. Alcoholism is marked by:

- Periods of preoccupation with alcohol (for example, "I can't wait until after work to get out and have a drink?")
- Impaired control over alcohol intake
- Continued use of alcohol despite adverse consequences or problems caused by drinking
- Distortion in thinking (most notably denial, minimization and rationalization).
- Alcoholics develop "tolerance" to alcohol, meaning they must drink more alcohol to feel its effects
- They may experience withdrawal symptoms such as shakiness, a more rapid pulse, sleep problems and even seizures when they try to stop drinking.

Talking to an alcoholic or alcohol abuser

The first, crucial step is to help alcoholics or alcohol abusers recognize that alcohol is at least a part of many of their problems. Following are some time-tested suggestions that are components of the ARISE method:

Raising the subject—There is no perfect time or place to bring up the issue, but do not do it while the person is drunk or drinking. Wait until he or she is sober. Sometimes a confrontation is more productive when facilitated by a professional who is knowledgeable about alcoholism and alcohol abuse and who can arrange a therapeutic "intervention."

Explaining the consequences—The following message should be kind but firm: The alcoholic or alcohol abuser needs to get help or suffer the consequences. Such consequences may include loss of job, chronic diseases, divorce, breakup of family or friendships, and most important you will no longer cover up for them.

Don't be brushed off—If you are seriously concerned about a person's drinking, do not allow him/her to distract your concerns. If you are constantly bailing the person out of trouble or giving him/her a "second chance," this pattern is likely to be interpreted by an alcoholic or alcohol abuser as permission to keep drinking.

Blame is counterproductive—Someone with an alcohol problem is likely to feel misunderstood. Try to put blame aside because it only feeds such feelings. Remember that alcohol addiction is a disease, not a moral weakness.

One-on-One the alcoholic always wins—It is common to become isolated in the effort of trying to get the alcoholic help. Once you are isolated into one-on-one confrontations the alcoholic almost always wins. The alcoholic, in one-on-one interactions, has the power to manipulate with promises and short-term efforts to improve, then blaming you as the cause of the problem. It is important to build a support network, such an intervention group, in order to avoid the pitfalls of getting caught in a one-on-one confrontation.

Don't wait until it's too late—Putting off the discussion or confrontation increases the risk of serious health and social problems. As with any disease, the earlier the treatment, the better. The alcoholic does not have to "hit bottom" in order to get help.

Don't neglect your own needs—It's easy for the alcohol problems of one person to overwhelm an entire family. There often are a series of family or personal stresses that show up in emotional, economic, physical, and social functioning from living with alcoholism. You may feel anger, resentment, depression, betrayal and disillusionment. Counseling may be necessary to help you understand alcoholism and learn appropriate actions for your own well-being. Intervention is a proven method to both get you support and to help a loved one get started in treatment. One way to help the alcoholic or alcohol abuser is to attend to your own needs and those of other family members. Going to alcohol support groups such as Al-Anon can be very helpful.

The ARISE method builds on the above points. Working with a Certified ARISE Interventionist will support you in building an intervention group (so you are not going at it alone) and to successfully help your loved one get started in treatment. The above points can be applied to all addictive behaviors, including, drug abuse, sexual addiction, Internet addiction, and eating disorders. The focus on alcoholism is meant as an illustration using the most common addiction.

Sample Letters From Family Members:

1. Letter from Intervention Network to Addicted Individual after First Meeting that s/he did not attend.

Dear Alex,

We are writing to you due to our concerns that come from issues from your alcohol and drug use. As you know, we had a meeting that you were invited to attend. This letter is because we want to let you know how we feel and what our concerns are. We have learned a great deal about alcoholism and addiction and we have two different perspectives at this time. Your choices will ultimately determine which perspective will turn out to be true.

From Mom:

As you know, my father (your grandfather) was an alcoholic. My concern is this disease has been passed onto you. I know there are only three outcomes from this disease: jail, death or hopefully, recovery. I pray that you will choose recovery for your life because I could not bear the other two alternatives. I want you to know I will always be there for you in my prayers and thoughts, regardless of what your choice is. However, you have my complete commitment of support if you choose to go into counseling and get help with this disease. I know you think this is something you can control on your own, but I know from personal experience that you need professional help to combat this disease. I hope you prove me wrong.

From Dad:

First there are some things about myself that I may not have told you before. When I was your age, I was involved with drugs and I regularly used them. At the time, I didn't think that there would be any harm, but as I became older, I realized that the world is a very difficult place to succeed in and that most companies will not tolerate drug or alcohol use. When I was about your age, I started to get bored with the same bad habits and I realized that if I wanted to move on with my life, I could not continue to do drugs.

I know that you are in a point in your life where you are around drug and alcohol use and I have seen many of the problems that you have had to deal with, because of your use. For instance, you were suspended and I believe ultimately dropped out of High School due to drug use. You were unable to work for CSX because you failed the drug test, and you recently have lost your license due to a DUI, to name a few problems. I hope you can realize that these problems could indicate that you may be afflicted by an addiction. Since I also used at your age, I hope that you will be able to stop soon, so that you will move on with your life. I have faith in you that you will be able to stop on your own, just as I did. Just think how much the drug and alcohol use has cost you so far.

We would like your agreement in the next step. Would you agree to attend a meeting with the three of us, including Sue if a problem occurs in the future that is alcohol or drug related? The purpose of this meeting would be to discuss options to help you in an open way.

Love,

Mom, Dad and Sue

2. Letter to spouse (constructed in a Level II meeting with the full support of the Intervention Network) when the Addicted Individual did not attend and a new problem surfaced between the meetings.

Dear Jerry,

Over the past month you have exemplified behavior that has proven to me your interest and commitment to being an active father to Shelly and a committed partner to me. I thank you for being there at the hospital and helping me the whole last month. I couldn't have done it without you.

In light of the events on Monday with your drinking and driving with Shelly in the car, I am forced to take action to prevent this from ever happening again. Under no circumstances are you to take Shelly in the car with you by yourself. I am letting all of your family and my family know about this ground rule and that it applies either locally or if Shelly is visiting in Syracuse. I will only consider changing this ground rule if you have stopped drinking and have stable recovery through participation in a treatment program.

I know I am powerless over your drinking. It hurts me a great deal to see that you are choosing alcohol over your family and our love for you. You are in my prayers. I love you and want only the best for you. Please make the right decision—you have our support. My dream is for us to raise Shelly as a married couple.

Love,

Debbie and Shelly

3. Letter to father from adult children after father left a Level II meeting, encouraging him not to give up and to be more open and less ashamed. Note the adult children's commitment to the process and addressing their father where he is regarding his drinking, yet also holding him accountable.

Dear Dad,

We are more worried about you than ever. We understand that you are having medical problems with an ulcer. We remember our last family session when you came after drinking and then went outside with Jim who saw the Mike's Lemonade bottles in the carrier next to your driver seat. You had denied drinking and driving in our earlier family sessions. The drinking is more of a problem than you are admitting.

We have talked to medical professionals about whether you could be doing additional harm to yourself by continuing to drink when you have an ulcer. Has your Doctor ever warned you not to drink because you have an ulcer? We have been told that this type of warning is standard medical practice.

We are looking forward to being with you at your retirement party to celebrate your hard work and dedication to supporting our family. We know you have made many sacrifices over the years for us. We are so proud of you and so thankful for your strong work ethic.

We are also aware that there will be an open bar at your party. We would prefer that you not drink at all that night due to your health problems. However, we can understand that you would want to drink that night to join in the celebration. If you are planning to drink that night we want to plan ahead and arrange to pick you up and take you back home. We'll be the designated driver for the whole night. That would mean we would need to know where you are now living.

You have been secretive with us about where you are now living. We believe that means you are living with a woman. We've been to the last two places you have been living—we don't understand why you are hiding this from us now. We love you, accept you and want you to be happy, even dating another woman. You don't have to hide this from us and you need to know that we would not tell Mom.

We know you left the last meeting upset. You need to know how much we love you. We've had really nice times getting together over the last two months. Please Dad, let's continue to meet and continue to move forward. The past is in the past. We don't think you are a bad father. Think about it, if we thought you were such a bad father, why would we be making such an effort to get together with you.

We'll talk to plan the details around the retirement party.

Love,

Sam and Doug

OTHER WEB RESOURCES:

Alcoholics Anonymous
www.alcoholics-anonymous.org

Alanon and Alateen
www.al-anon.org

Adult Children of Alcoholics
www.adultchildren.org

Co-Dependents Anonymous
www.codependents.org

Debtors Anonymous
www.debtorsanonymous.org

Emotions Anonymous
www.emotionsanonymous.org

Families Anonymous
www.familiesanonymous.org

Gamblers Anonymous
www.gamblersanonymous.org

Marijuana Anonymous
www.marijuana-anonymous.org

Narcotics Anonymous
www.na.org

Overeaters Anonymous
www.overeatersanonymous.org

Sex Addicts Anonymous
www.sexaa.org

Sex and Love Addicts Anonymous
www.slaafws.org

National Assoc. for Children of Alcoholics
www.health.org/nacoa

National Institute on Drug Abuse
www.nida.nih.gov

National Institute on Alcoholism and
Alcohol Abuse
www.niaaa.nih.gov

Substance Abuse and Mental Health
Services Administration
www.ncadi.samhsa.gov/dbases/nsawi

National Council on Alcoholism and
Drug Dependence
www.ncadd.org

Project CORK
http://www.projectcork.org

Robert Wood Johnson Foundation
www.rwjf.org

Rutgers Institute
www.rci.rutgers.edu

Columbia Univ. Substance Abuse Center
www.casacolumbia.org

About Recovery
www.alcoholism.about.com

BOOKS

Barth, Richard P., Pietrzak, J., & Ramler, M., Families Living with Drugs and HIV. Guilford Press, New York, NY, 1993

Black, C., (2003). Straight Talk: What Recovering Parents Should Tell their Kids about Drugs and Alcohol. Published by Hazelden.

Ketcham, K., Asbury, W. F., Ciaramicoli, Arthur P & Schulstad, Mel. (2000). Beyond the Influence: Understanding and Defeating Alcoholism.

Ketcham K. & Pace, N.A., Teens Under the Influence. Ballantine Books, New York, NY, 2003

Kuhn, C. & Swartzwelder, S., & Wilson, W., Buzzed. W.W. Norton and Co., New York, NY, 1998.

Kurtz, E. & Ketcham, K., The Spirituality of Imperfection. Bantam Publishing, New York, NY, 1994.

Miller, W. & Rollnick, S., Motivational Interviewing, Preparing People to Change Addictive Behavior. Guilford Press, New York, NY, 1991.

Sells, S., Treating the Tough Adolescent. Guilford Press, New York, NY, 1998.

Treadway, D., Before It's Too Late, Working With Substance Abuse in the Family. W.W. Norton and Co., New York, NY, 1989.

DR. JUDITH LANDAU AND JAMES GARRETT

APPENDIX C

ASSOCIATION OF ARISE INTERVENTIONITS

Association of Certified ARISE Interventionists (ACAI)

Eligibility:

Successful completion of the Certified ARISE Interventionist training

Annual Dues:

$225.00

Membership Benefits:

- Password protected community discussion forum for ARISE Interventionists (see below)
- Password protected community discussion forum for your ARISE families
- Template or Electronic file of official business cards
- Reduced price for ARISE brochures
- Reduced rates for consultation
- One additional hour of case consultation by telephone
- ARISE book for lay public 20% discount
- Reduced fees from the Distance Learning Center for all continuing education courses
- Reduced fees for the ARISE re-certification course

Password access from the web site (LinkingHumanSystems.com) to the Association of Certified ARISE Interventionists (ACAI) members only page includes the following benefits:

- Interactive case consultation
- Ongoing discussion with questions from ARISE Certified Interventionists and answers from trainers
- Case scenarios of successes and challenges shared by Interventionists
- Chat room with other ARISE Certified Interventionists
- Summaries of the latest research and publications related to intervention
- Profiles of other ACAI members
- Examples of "real world" applications of ARISE in both agency and private practice settings
- Updated outreach, networking and marketing ideas

INVITATIONAL INTERVENTION

Association of Certified ARISE Interventionists (ACAI)

Membership Application

Name:

Address for Web Site:

Address for mailing:
(if different)

Telephone for Web Site):

Telephone (not for publication):

FAX:

Email address:

Employer (name and address):

Professional Degrees:

Professional licenses or credentials:

I understand that in order to become a member of ACAI, I will be expected to pay annual
dues of $225.00. I also understand that I will be entitled to benefits shown on the reverse
side, which may be modified or changed from time to time at the sole discretion of
Linking Human Systems, LLC. This application shall not be deemed accepted unless and
until countersigned by an officer of Linking Human Systems, LLC.

Date: _____   Date: _____

_____   _____
Applicant Signature: Linking Human Systems, LLC

231269